STRONGER EVERY DAY FOR MEN

STRONGER EVERY DAY FOR MEN

365 Devotions

TYNDALE
MOMENTUM®

A Tyndale nonfiction imprint

Visit Tyndale online at tyndale.com.

Stronger Every Day for Men: 365 Devotions

Previously published in 2005 as *The One Year Mini for Men* by Tyndale House Publishers under ISBN 978-1-4143-0618-6.

General editors: Ronald A. Beers, Linda Taylor

Contributing editors: Rebecca Beers, Amy Mason, Christopher Mason

Contributing writers: V. Gilbert Beers, Ronald A. Beers, Brian R. Coffey, Jonathan Farrar, Jonathan Gray, Shawn A. Harrison, Sandy Hull, Rhonda K. O'Brien, Douglas J. Rumford

Designed by Libby Dykstra

Edited by Linda Schlafer

For information about special discounts for bulk purchases, please contact Tyndale House Publishers at csresponse@tyndale.com, or call 1-855-277-9400.

Library of Congress Cataloging-in-Publication Data

A catalog record for this book is available from the Library of Congress.

ISBN 979-8-4005-0089-3

Printed in the United States of America

30 29 28 27 26 25 24
7   6   5   4   3   2   1

FRESH START

Is it really possible for me to get a fresh start?

GOD'S RESPONSE

Create in me a clean heart, O God. Renew a right spirit within me.   *Psalm 51:10*

Do not despise these small beginnings, for the LORD rejoices to see the work begin.   *Zechariah 4:10*

YOU HARVEST WHAT YOU PLANT. Sunflower seeds produce sunflowers. Pumpkin seeds produce pumpkins. So if you ask God to plant a clean heart in you, your life will produce clean thoughts, actions, and motives. Bad desires and thoughts that remain are evidence that the enemy has planted some bad seeds and you need to do some weeding. Complete renewal has not yet been accomplished. No one will be entirely pure in this life, but purity of mind and heart is one of the most worthy goals to pursue this year. Is it your goal? How will you be different at the end of this year—inside and out—if you meet that goal?

GOD'S PROMISE

I am sure that God, who began the good work within you, will continue his work until it is finally finished on that day when Christ Jesus comes back again.
Philippians 1:6

VISION

Why is it important for me to seek God's vision for the future?

GOD'S RESPONSE

Glory be to God! By his mighty power at work within us, he is able to accomplish infinitely more than we would ever dare to ask or hope.   *Ephesians 3:20*

The truth is, anyone who believes in me will do the same works I have done, and even greater works, because I am going to be with the Father.   *John 14:12*

YOU ALREADY HAVE SOME VISION of the future. Seeking God's vision breaks your bondage to small ideas that are not worthy of God or representative of God's work in the world. God's vision inspires hope in greater possibilities. By aligning your vision with God's vision for your life, you will be able to navigate your future with purpose and clarity.

GOD'S CHALLENGE

"My thoughts are completely different from yours," says the LORD. "And my ways are far beyond anything you could imagine. For just as the heavens are higher than the earth, so are my ways higher than your ways and my thoughts higher than your thoughts."   *Isaiah 55:8-9*

VISION

How can I align my vision with God's plan for me?

GOD'S RESPONSE

Elisha prayed, "O LORD, open his eyes and let him see!" The LORD opened his servant's eyes, and when he looked up, he saw that the hillside around Elisha was filled with horses and chariots of fire.   *2 Kings 6:17*

Because I have done what is right, I will see you. When I awake, I will be fully satisfied, for I will see you face to face.   *Psalm 17:15*

Open my eyes to see the wonderful truths in your law. *Psalm 119:18*

THERE ARE SEVERAL WAYS TO FIND God's vision for your life: through his Word, through the conscience he has built into you, through the counsel of other godly people, and through prayer. God wants to reveal his vision for your life. Believe in his power, seek his guidance each day, and be alert to the ways that he answers you.

GOD'S PROMISE

God blesses those whose hearts are pure, for they will see God.   *Matthew 5:8*

INFLUENCE

Can I really make a difference in the world?

GOD'S RESPONSE

Those who look to him for help will be radiant with joy; no shadow of shame will darken their faces. *Psalm 34:5*

"It is not by force nor by strength, but by my Spirit, says the Lord Almighty." *Zechariah 4:6*

I have called you back from the ends of the earth so you can serve me. For I have chosen you. *Isaiah 41:9*

G OD HAS A PLAN THAT IS JUST FOR YOU—a purpose for your life that no one else can fill. God also knows that you are limited and need his help. Acknowledge God's authority each day by confessing your need for him, honor God by consulting him in prayer, seek wisdom in his Word, and then consider whether your actions are consistent with what you have read. God will guide you. Since God made you with such a specific purpose in mind, he will surely help you become a man that makes a difference in the world.

GOD'S CHALLENGE

Jesus explained, "I tell you the truth, the Son can do nothing by himself. He does only what he sees the Father doing. Whatever the Father does, the Son also does." *John 5:19* (NLT2)

GOALS

Why is it important for me to set goals?

GOD'S RESPONSE

Even I, the Son of Man, came here not to be served but to serve others, and to give my life as a ransom for many. *Mark 10:45*

I brought glory to you here on earth by doing everything you told me to do. *John 17:4*

A GOAL KEEPS YOU FOCUSED ON your primary mission and helps to structure your life. Jesus' goal of giving salvation shaped the way he lived every day and guided his every interaction with others. We are often tempted to do too much, but God gives us only what we can accomplish while living a godly, balanced life. God is not glorified by our doing everything we can possibly do, but by our fulfilling the specific tasks he has for us. What are God's goals for your life?

GOD'S CHALLENGE

I run straight to the goal with purpose in every step. I am not like a boxer who misses his punches. *1 Corinthians 9:26*

ABILITIES

How can I use my abilities for God?

GOD'S RESPONSE

God gave these four young men an unusual aptitude for learning the literature and science of the time.   *Daniel 1:17*

My life is worth nothing unless I use it for doing the work assigned me by the Lord Jesus.   *Acts 20:24*

G OD GIVES US ALL SPECIAL ABILITIES and spiritual gifts that he intends for us to develop and use. As you identify your gifts and abilities, you have three choices. First, you can ignore them. But this will leave you unfulfilled and disconnected from God's plan for you. Second, you can use them to advance your own goals and agenda. Third, you can put them to their intended use and maximize God's purpose for you. As you read and obey God's Word, you will begin to understand your special abilities and spiritual gifts. Using them to serve God will help you discover your distinctive role among his people and give you deep satisfaction.

GOD'S PROMISE

There are different ways God works in our lives, but it is the same God who does the work through all of us. A spiritual gift is given to each of us as a means of helping the entire church.   *1 Corinthians 12:6-7*

How should I pursue my goals?

GOD'S RESPONSE

If your aim is to enjoy this world, you can't be a friend of God.   *James 4:4*

Our aim is to please him always.   *2 Corinthians 5:9*

GOALS SET THE AGENDA FOR YOUR DAY, your week, your year, and your life. Goals also set the direction in which you move. Therefore, it's important to have the right goals so your life will go in the right direction. As you determine your goals for this coming year, make them more than just urgent tasks to check off of a "to do" list. Make them assignments with a purpose. Do your goals align you with God's Word or contradict it? Are your goals in keeping with your special abilities and spiritual gifts? Are your goals, even the small ones, honoring God? If so, you are headed in the right direction and your accomplishments will be meaningful.

GOD'S CHALLENGE

Since we are surrounded by such a huge crowd of witnesses to the life of faith, let us strip off every weight that slows us down, especially the sin that so easily hinders our progress. And let us run with endurance the race that God has set before us.   *Hebrews 12:1*

CALLING

How can I know God's call for my life?

GOD'S RESPONSE

Let God transform you into a new person by changing the way you think. Then you will know what God wants you to do.   *Romans 12:2*

Cry out for insight and understanding. Search for them as you would for lost money or hidden treasure. Then you will understand what it means to fear the LORD, and you will gain knowledge of God.   *Proverbs 2:3-5*

THE FIRST STEP IN KNOWING your calling is to tune your ears to hear God when he calls. Just as a piano is tuned against a standard set of musical notes, so we get in tune with God as we examine our lives against the standards for living found in the Bible. As God communicates to you through the Bible, you will begin to "hear," or discern, just what he wants of you. As your spiritual hearing is enhanced, you will become a good listener, able to hear clearly when God calls you to a certain task that he has reserved just for you. Would God say that you are a good listener?

GOD'S PROMISE

Your word is a lamp for my feet and a light for my path.
Psalm 119:105

PROVISION

What does God provide so I can fulfill his call?

GOD'S RESPONSE

May the God of peace . . . equip you with all you need for doing his will. May he produce in you, through the power of Jesus Christ, all that is pleasing to him.   *Hebrews 13:20*

All Scripture is inspired by God. . . . It is God's way of preparing us in every way, fully equipped for every good thing God wants us to do.   *2 Timothy 3:16-17*

When the Holy Spirit has come upon you, you will receive power.   *Acts 1:8*

WHEN GOD CALLS US TO A TASK, he equips us for it. If you have tuned yourself to hear his call, you can be sure he will give you the resources to fulfill it. He has given you his Word for counsel and direction. God has given you special abilities and gifts to use in your calling. He has sent his Holy Spirit to give you strength and guidance.

GOD'S PROMISE

May the God of peace make you holy in every way, and may your whole spirit and soul and body be kept blameless until that day when our Lord Jesus Christ comes again. God, who calls you, is faithful; he will do this.   *1 Thessalonians 5:23-24*

JOURNEY

Does God have a specific plan for my life?
Can I mess it up?

GOD'S RESPONSE

God's gifts and his call can never be withdrawn.
Romans 11:29

The LORD will work out his plans for my life.   *Psalm 138:8*

G OD'S PLAN FOR YOUR LIFE is not a written script that
  you must follow; rather, it is a journey with various
important destinations and appointments, but also a great
deal of freedom as to the pace and scope of the travel.
God's plan for you will always have a sense of mystery
about it, but you can be certain that as you seek his leading, God will guide and direct you on your journey. Most
of God's promises are conditional. In other words, they
depend on something that you are asked to do. If you
separate yourself from God, you are removing yourself
from his plan, his guidance, and his promises. Come back
to him, and he will redeem your lost time.

GOD'S PROMISE

We know that God causes everything to work together
for the good of those who love God and are called
according to his purpose for them.   *Romans 8:28*

UNCERTAINTY

What can I be sure of when I'm faced with the unknown?

GOD'S RESPONSE

The LORD says, "I will guide you along the best pathway for your life. I will advise you and watch over you."
Psalm 32:8

A voice from heaven called to me: "Keep secret what the seven thunders said. Do not write it down."
Revelation 10:4

WHEN YOU ARE FACED WITH THE UNKNOWN, keep doing what you know to do: love others, worship God, obey his Word, and work on strengthening your character. The Bible says that God will show you the next step when you need it. God does not reveal everything about his will for you, but he does reveal everything you need to know to live for him now. You can trust him with each next step.

GOD'S PROMISE

I know the plans I have for you. . . . They are plans for good and not for disaster, to give you a future and a hope.
Jeremiah 29:11

WORRY

Can I really trust God with my future?

GOD'S RESPONSE

Here on earth you will have many trials and sorrows. But take heart, because I have overcome the world. *John 16:33*

Don't worry about tomorrow, for tomorrow will bring its own worries. Today's trouble is enough for today. *Matthew 6:34*

YOU CAN TRUST GOD WITH YOUR FUTURE because you have a faithful God who loves you and promises to guide you to a perfect, eternal future if you follow him. Jesus never promised a problem-free life; in fact, he guaranteed that life would not be easy. So don't be surprised by hard times and don't be afraid of them. There is no problem that Jesus can't handle or overcome. Many of the things that you are afraid might happen never do, so don't waste time on "what-if" worries, for either the past or the future. Turn your worry time into prayer time.

GOD'S PROMISE

The LORD keeps watch over you as you come and go, both now and forever.   *Psalm 121:8*

*I'm afraid that if I trust God, he will
take me someplace I don't want to go.
What can I do about this fear?*

GOD'S RESPONSE

Take delight in the LORD, and he will give you your heart's
desires.　*Psalm 37:4*

My purpose is to give life in all its fullness.　*John 10:10*

May he grant your heart's desire and fulfill all your plans.
Psalm 20:4

"For I know the plans I have for you," says the LORD.
"They are plans for good and not for disaster, to give you
a future and a hope."　*Jeremiah 29:11*

GOD'S PLANS ARE ALWAYS GOOD PLANS. His desires
for you will fulfill and satisfy you. If your mind and
heart are truly in tune with his will, you won't be going
where you don't want to go. He changes your heart before
he adjusts your future plans. Will you let him change your
heart? Since God alone knows the future, who can plan
your future better than he?

GOD'S PROMISE

He fills my life with good things.　*Psalm 103:5*

RISK

What kind of risk is involved in following God?

GOD'S RESPONSE

"Now go, for I am sending you to Pharaoh. You will lead my people, the Israelites, out of Egypt."

"But who am I to appear before Pharaoh?" Moses asked God. "How can you expect me to lead the Israelites out of Egypt?" *Exodus 3:10-11*

Mary responded, "I am the Lord's servant, and I am willing to accept whatever he wants. May everything you have said come true." *Luke 1:38*

WHEN GOD ASKS YOU TO FOLLOW HIM, he often doesn't give all the information about what is happening right away. When you step out in faith, he gives guidance as you go. Moses risked his life by approaching Pharaoh and leading the Israelites out of captivity. Mary risked her marriage, her reputation, and her future by becoming the mother of Jesus. Following God's will is not without risks; the only thing more risky than trusting God is not trusting him!

GOD'S PROMISE

Guide my steps by your word, so I will not be overcome by any evil. *Psalm 119:133*

What should be the basis for risk-taking?

GOD'S RESPONSE

What is faith? It is the confident assurance that what we hope for is going to happen. It is the evidence of things we cannot yet see. God gave his approval to people in days of old because of their faith. . . . It was by faith that Noah built an ark to save his family from the flood. . . . It was by faith that Abraham obeyed when God called him to leave home and go to another land that God would give him as his inheritance. *Hebrews 11:1-2, 7-8*

NO GREAT THINGS HAPPEN without some risk. Noah risked his reputation by believing that God would flood the earth as he had said he would. Abraham left his home and country to go where God sent him. Those who walk close to God have evidence based on their past experiences that God is real and active in the lives of those who love him. God loves to accomplish the impossible in the lives of his people. Take him up on it.

GOD'S CHALLENGE

Jesus told him, "You believe because you have seen me. Blessed are those who haven't seen me and believe anyway." *John 20:29*

RISK

What must a risk-taker be prepared to do?

GOD'S RESPONSE

Two of the men who had explored the land, Joshua son of Nun and Caleb son of Jephunneh, tore their clothing. They said to the community of Israel, "The land we explored is a wonderful land! And if the Lord is pleased with us, he will bring us safely into that land and give it to us. . . . Don't be afraid of them!"   *Numbers 14:6-9*

YOU SHOULD BE READY TO RISK your resources, reputation, and even some relationships in order to be faithful to God. Joshua and Caleb, unlike the other spies, were willing to risk everything because they trusted God's promises more than their human fears. God had already promised the Israelites the land; all they had to do was take it. God has made many promises in his Word for his people. Will you take the risk of moving ahead and claiming them, or will you lose heart and miss the blessings God has in store for you?

GOD'S PROMISE

Caleb . . . will see this land because he has followed the Lord completely. I will give to him and his descendants some of the land he walked over during his scouting mission.   *Deuteronomy 1:36*

CAUTION

What are some cautions I should be aware of when it comes to risk-taking?

GOD'S RESPONSE

Trusting oneself is foolish, but those who walk in wisdom are safe.   *Proverbs 28:26*

Fools think they need no advice, but the wise listen to others.   *Proverbs 12:15*

The wise are cautious and avoid danger; fools plunge ahead with great confidence.   *Proverbs 14:16*

THERE IS A DIFFERENCE between being a risk-taker and being a fool. The Bible warns us not to take risks that ignore or contradict sound principles. Consulting God and wise friends committed to God before taking big steps in life provides a high chance of success. Fools rarely consult others, never consult God, and make plans that are mostly for personal gain or fame. God is looking for wise and obedient risk-takers, not foolish people who plunge ahead without first seeking his guidance.

GOD'S CHALLENGE

Since fools base their thoughts on foolish premises, their conclusions will be wicked madness.   *Ecclesiastes 10:13*

WISDOM

How can I gain wisdom?

GOD'S RESPONSE

Teach me your ways, O LORD, that I may live according to your truth! Grant me purity of heart, that I may honor you.   *Psalm 86:11*

Lead me in the right path, O LORD. . . . Tell me clearly what to do, and show me which way to turn.   *Psalm 5:8*

If you need wisdom—if you want to know what God wants you to do—ask him, and he will gladly tell you. He will not resent your asking.   *James 1:5*

GIVING GOD FIRST PLACE IN YOUR LIFE is a prerequisite to receiving his wisdom. God promises to give wisdom to anyone who asks, but asking God for wisdom is hollow if you are not willing to give God control of your heart. Wisdom comes from the Holy Spirit who lives in those who believe in Christ. Thus wisdom is found in relationship with God.

GOD'S CHALLENGE

The fear of the Lord is true wisdom; to forsake evil is real understanding.   *Job 28:28*

WISDOM

How will having wisdom help me in my life?

GOD'S RESPONSE

Since a dull ax requires great strength, sharpen the blade. That's the value of wisdom; it helps you succeed.
Ecclesiastes 10:10

Give me an understanding mind so that I . . . know the difference between right and wrong.   *1 Kings 3:9*

WISDOM ISN'T JUST KNOWING THE FACTS—it is understanding that an all-powerful, all-knowing God has designed a moral standard in which both good and sinful choices have consequences. Wisdom also means choosing to apply God's truth and principles in your relationships and daily circumstances. Wisdom begins with understanding your accountability to your creator and with choosing to depend fully on him. Wisdom isn't just what you know, but how you live.

GOD'S PROMISE

Wisdom will multiply your days and add years to your life. If you become wise, you will be the one to benefit. If you scorn wisdom, you will be the one to suffer.
Proverbs 9:11-12

WISDOM

Is there any wisdom apart from God?
Is he the only source of wisdom?

GOD'S RESPONSE

Don't be impressed with your own wisdom. Instead, fear the LORD and turn your back on evil.   *Proverbs 3:7*

In him lie hidden all the treasures of wisdom and knowledge.   *Colossians 2:3*

The wisdom of this world is foolishness to God. As the Scriptures say, "God catches those who think they are wise in their own cleverness."   *1 Corinthians 3:19*

TRUE WISDOM COMES FROM GOD. Although God may use other resources—such as the world he created or other people—to provide you with his wisdom, be careful to evaluate these other sources. While they may seem insightful or able to offer good advice at times, screen everything against the wise words of God recorded in the Bible. When you read the truth every day, you will get better at discerning the lies of the evil one.

GOD'S PROMISE

By wisdom the LORD founded the earth; by understanding he established the heavens.   *Proverbs 3:19*

TRUST

What makes God trustworthy?

GOD'S RESPONSE

He passed in front of Moses and said, "I am the LORD, I am the LORD, the merciful and gracious God. I am slow to anger and rich in unfailing love and faithfulness." *Exodus 34:6*

This truth gives them the confidence of eternal life, which God promised them before the world began—and he cannot lie.   *Titus 1:2*

Those who know your name trust in you, for you, O LORD, have never abandoned anyone who searches for you.   *Psalm 9:10*

YOU CAN TRUST GOD because he is the source of truth. How do you know? Because nothing he has said in his Word, the Bible, has ever been proven wrong or false. Every prophecy that is not still in the future has been fulfilled. The source of truth cannot tell a lie.

GOD'S PROMISE

Your unfailing love will last forever. Your faithfulness is as enduring as the heavens.   *Psalm 89:2*

SALVATION

How can I know that I am truly saved?

GOD'S RESPONSE

For all who are led by the Spirit of God are children of God.   *Romans 8:14*

To all who believed him and accepted him, he gave the right to become children of God.   *John 1:12*

GOD PROMISES THAT YOU WILL BE SAVED from eternal punishment if you believe in your heart that Jesus Christ is the Son of God, that he died to take the punishment for your sins, and that he rose from the dead to conquer death forever. If you confess that you are a sinner who needs God, ask God to forgive your sins, and accept Jesus Christ as Lord of your life (i.e., give him control of your life), then you can be sure that you are truly saved. You will live for eternity in heaven, and you will also experience a spiritual rebirth now—a new and abundant life guided by the wisdom of God's Holy Spirit.

GOD'S PROMISE

If you confess with your mouth that Jesus is Lord and believe in your heart that God raised him from the dead, you will be saved.   *Romans 10:9*

WARRIOR GOD

What kind of God am I trusting?

GOD'S RESPONSE

The LORD himself will fight for you. You won't have to lift a finger in your defense!   *Exodus 14:14*

The LORD is a warrior; yes, the LORD is his name!
Exodus 15:3

Each one of you will put to flight a thousand of the enemy, for the LORD your God fights for you, just as he has promised.   *Joshua 23:10*

YOU ARE TRUSTING A GOD who is a mighty warrior, always ready to fight on your behalf. When enemies come against you, they come against the Lord as well. Ultimate victory is assured when you let the Lord fight your battles. He often turns your enemies against each other so that they destroy themselves while you walk away unscathed.

GOD'S PROMISE

The LORD stands beside me like a great warrior. Before him they will stumble. They cannot defeat me. They will be shamed and thoroughly humiliated. Their dishonor will never be forgotten.   *Jeremiah 20:11*

BATTLES

How does God help me in my daily battles?

GOD'S RESPONSE

Whenever you were in distress and turned to the LORD . . . and sought him out, you found him.   *2 Chronicles 15:4*

He is your protecting shield and your triumphant sword! *Deuteronomy 33:29*

The LORD is my strength, my shield from every danger. I trust in him with all my heart. He helps me, and my heart is filled with joy.   *Psalm 28:7*

P RAYER IS THE LIFELINE that connects you to God. His Holy Spirit, who is with you at all times, helps you to pray even when you don't know what to say or how to ask for help. No matter what kind of battle you must fight today, think of God's presence as your protecting shield and your triumphant sword.

GOD'S PROMISE

The Lord is my helper, so I will not be afraid. What can mere mortals do to me?   *Hebrews 13:6*

ARMOR

How does God arm me for my daily battles?

GOD'S RESPONSE

Put on all of God's armor so that you will be able to stand firm against all strategies and tricks of the Devil. For we are not fighting against people made of flesh and blood, but against the evil rulers and authorities of the unseen world, against those mighty powers of darkness who rule this world, and against wicked spirits in the heavenly realms. Use every piece of God's armor to resist the enemy in the time of evil, so that after the battle you will still be standing firm. Stand your ground, putting on the sturdy belt of truth and the body armor of God's righteousness. For shoes, put on the peace that comes from the Good News, so that you will be fully prepared. In every battle you will need faith as your shield to stop the fiery arrows aimed at you by Satan. Put on salvation as your helmet, and take the sword of the Spirit, which is the word of God. Pray at all times and on every occasion in the power of the Holy Spirit. *Ephesians 6:11-18*

I F YOU WANT TO BE A MIGHTY WARRIOR for God, you must learn to use all of these spiritual weapons.

GOD'S CHALLENGE

Clothe yourselves with the armor of right living, as those who live in the light. *Romans 13:12*

TRUTH

How will the truth help me fight my battles?

GOD'S RESPONSE

Stand your ground, putting on the sturdy belt of truth.
Ephesians 6:14

You will know the truth, and the truth will set you free.
John 8:32

When the Spirit of truth comes, he will guide you into all
truth. He will not be presenting his own ideas; he will be
telling you what he has heard. He will tell you about the
future.   *John 16:13*

WHEN YOU BELIEVE THE TRUTH taught in God's Word
and live it out, you will have the upper hand in any
battle against evil. You must be loyal to God and ask him for
help. When you do this, he will give you great discernment
as well as protection against Satan and his demons that are
fighting even now for your soul. The Word of God and the
Holy Spirit are mighty resources that can overpower your
enemy. Stand strong and confident in your faith, and you
can be certain that God will help you fight your battles so
that you will be victorious.

GOD'S PROMISE

Jesus told him, "I am . . . the truth."   *John 14:6*

RIGHTEOUSNESS

How can I be righteous when I'm in the middle of a battle?

GOD'S RESPONSE

Stand your ground, putting on . . . the body armor of God's righteousness.   *Ephesians 6:14*

We are made right in God's sight when we trust in Jesus Christ to take away our sins. And we all can be saved in this same way, no matter who we are or what we have done.   *Romans 3:22*

A S A BELIEVER, you have been made righteous in God's eyes because Jesus forgave your sin when you confessed it to him. You may be tempted to think you're not good enough, but God looks at you as if you have no sin. He sees the abilities and gifts he created in you. You can confidently stand your ground against temptation and evil because God is fighting for you. When you are equipped with the armor of God and God is at your side, Satan cannot defeat you.

GOD'S CHALLENGE

I no longer count on my own goodness or my ability to obey God's law, but I trust Christ to save me. For God's way of making us right with himself depends on faith. *Philippians 3:9*

PEACE

How can I find peace in the midst of my battles?

GOD'S RESPONSE

For shoes, put on the peace that comes from the Good News, so that you will be fully prepared.   *Ephesians 6:15*

If you do this, you will experience God's peace, which is far more wonderful than the human mind can understand. His peace will guard your hearts and minds as you live in Christ Jesus.   *Philippians 4:7*

TO PUT ON PEACE MEANS THAT YOU ARE READY for any battle because you are confident in the knowledge that you are on the winning side. When Satan disturbs you through trials and temptations, you can face your challenges with composure and with the confidence that comes from knowing that your salvation and your future are secure.

GOD'S CHALLENGE

How beautiful on the mountains are the feet of those who bring good news of peace and salvation, the news that the God of Israel reigns!   *Isaiah 52:7*

SHIELD

Sometimes it feels like I'm under attack.
How does God defend me?

GOD'S RESPONSE

In every battle you will need faith as your shield to stop the fiery arrows aimed at you by Satan.   *Ephesians 6:16*

The Spirit who lives in you is greater than the spirit who lives in the world.   *1 John 4:4*

Every child of God defeats this evil world by trusting Christ to give the victory.   *1 John 5:4*

YOUR FIRST LINE OF DEFENSE is to draw strength from the fact that God is more powerful than your problems or your enemies. Your faith in God is a shield that protects you from the temptations and criticisms hurled at you every day. Without strong faith, the weapons of Satan and the arrows shot at you by your enemies would pierce and defeat you. So even when life seems overwhelming, hold tightly to your faith like a shield and you will withstand the dangers and discouragements sent at you. And rejoice—you know that God has already won the victory.

GOD'S PROMISE

The LORD protects those of childlike faith; I was facing death, and then he saved me.   *Psalm 116:6*

SALVATION

I know I'm saved, but what does that mean in my everyday life?

GOD'S RESPONSE

Put on salvation as your helmet.   *Ephesians 6:17*

I will give you treasures hidden in the darkness—secret riches. I will do this so you may know that I am the LORD, the God of Israel, the one who calls you by name.   *Isaiah 45:3*

I write this to you who believe in the Son of God, so that you may know you have eternal life.   *1 John 5:13*

W HEN YOU PUT ON THE HELMET of salvation, you are deliberately protecting your head, and this is a powerful defense against troubles in this world. You live with a new perspective because when you trusted in Jesus Christ for salvation, the Holy Spirit began to change your mind. As he works within you, your way of thinking becomes more and more like that of Jesus and begins to stay focused on what is really important. This impacts every relationship you have and every decision you make.

GOD'S PROMISE

Those who become Christians become new persons. They are not the same anymore, for the old life is gone. A new life has begun!   *2 Corinthians 5:17*

DEFENSE

I've heard that the best defense is a good offense.
So how do I fight back?

GOD'S RESPONSE

Take the sword of the Spirit, which is the word of God.
Ephesians 6:17

Humble yourselves before God. Resist the Devil, and he
will flee from you.   *James 4:7*

YOUR OFFENSIVE WEAPON is the Word of God. It's odd
to think of the Bible as a weapon, but in it God reveals
his plan of attack against everything and everyone that tries to
bring you down. It is your battle plan; if you don't read it you
won't know how to fight the battle that literally determines
your destiny. Only by knowing whom you are fighting,
where the battle is, and how to defend yourself will you be
able to win. It is vital to read God's Word as regularly as possible. This is the weapon that sends Satan running for cover.

GOD'S CHALLENGE

For the word of God is full of living power. It is sharper
than the sharpest knife, cutting deep into our innermost
thoughts and desires. It exposes us for what we really are.
Hebrews 4:12

*How can the Bible—a book written so long ago—
be relevant for me today?*

GOD'S RESPONSE

The grass withers, and the flowers fade, but the word of
our God stands forever.   *Isaiah 40:8*

How can a young person stay pure? By obeying your word
and following its rules. . . . I have hidden your word in my
heart, that I might not sin against you.   *Psalm 119:9, 11*

THE BIBLE HAS STOOD THE TEST of time more than any
other document in human history. Because the Bible
is the Word of God, it is the only document that is "living,"
relevant for all people in all places for all time. People change
over time, but people's basic needs for love, acceptance, purpose, and fulfillment remain the same. The Bible addresses
all human needs. It is as contemporary as the heart of God
and more powerful than your most urgent need. It will sus-
tain you and bring you joy no matter what happens in life
because God is literally speaking to you through it.

GOD'S CHALLENGE

Even more blessed are all who hear the word of God and
put it into practice.   *Luke 11:28*

CONNECTION

How can I connect with God as I read his Word?

GOD'S RESPONSE

You will keep on guiding me with your counsel, leading me to a glorious destiny.   *Psalm 73:24*

Remember your promise to me, for it is my only hope. . . . It comforts me in all my troubles.   *Psalm 119:49-50*

They are a warning to those who hear them.   *Psalm 19:11*

W HEN YOU WANT TO BUILD A CONNECTION with other people, you begin by learning about them—who they are, what they do for a living, and what interests they have. If you share their interests, you will have a basis for a real connection with them. God's Word is his way of telling us about himself. By following God's Word, you will join God in bringing about his will, and you will establish a personal connection with him.

GOD'S CHALLENGE

They fill their hearts with God's law, so they will never slip from his path.   *Psalm 37:31*

HEART

What kind of heart does God desire for me?

GOD'S RESPONSE

You desire honesty from the heart, so you can teach me to be wise in my inmost being. . . . Create in me a clean heart, O God. Renew a right spirit within me.   *Psalm 51:6, 10*

G OD IS FAR MORE CONCERNED about the condition of our hearts than he is with our external behavior—for our behavior always flows from our hearts, and not the other way around. When our motives are selfish or impure, it is only a matter of time until our actions are also selfish and impure. To have the kind of heart God desires, you must first sincerely desire a relationship with him. This comes through a determination to live with integrity, to be humble, to obey God's Word, and to love and serve others. If your motives are good and you are really trying to do this, then God is pleased with your heart. He's not asking for perfection, just sincere effort.

GOD'S PROMISE

I will give them singleness of heart and put a new spirit within them. I will take away their hearts of stone and give them tender hearts instead, so they will obey my laws and regulations. Then they will truly be my people, and I will be their God.   *Ezekiel 11:19-20*

TENDERNESS

I want a tender heart, but I also want a strong and courageous heart. Can I have both?

GOD'S RESPONSE

Never before had there been a king like Josiah, who turned to the Lord with all his heart and soul and strength. *2 Kings 23:25*

Love the Lord your God, walk in all his ways, obey his commands, be faithful to him, and serve him with all your heart and all your soul. *Joshua 22:5*

A TENDER HEART IS NOT A WEAK HEART. Tenderness is the quiet, compassionate, persevering character trait that only comes through a refining process. When you have been through a lot of pain and have suffered hurt, you develop compassion and empathy for the hurts of others. Tenderness is powerful in its expression of compassion, yet gentle in the mercy it extends to those who need comfort and encouragement. Weakness lacks compassion and empathy. If you are truly tender, then you are able to be courageous and strong.

GOD'S PROMISE

You will have courage because you will have hope. *Job 11:18*

HUMILITY

What's the best way to serve God?

GOD'S RESPONSE

Your attitude should be the same that Christ Jesus had. Though he was God, he did not demand and cling to his rights as God. He made himself nothing; he took the humble position of a slave and appeared in human form. And in human form he obediently humbled himself even further by dying a criminal's death on a cross. *Philippians 2:5-8*

HUMILITY IS THE PATHWAY TO SERVICE. True humility results from understanding who you are and who God is. Humility allows you to serve wherever God places you and to do whatever God asks of you. A patient who regains health through a physician's care is more humble because he realizes his vulnerability. We are humbled when we realize how God heals our souls and provides all that we need. When we realize our dependence on him, we're happy to serve our Lord in any way he asks of us.

GOD'S CHALLENGE

So humble yourselves under the mighty power of God, and in his good time he will honor you.   *1 Peter 5:6*

HEART

Why does the Bible tell me to "guard" my heart?

GOD'S RESPONSE

Above all else, guard your heart, for it affects everything you do.   *Proverbs 4:23*

Dear children, keep away from anything that might take God's place in your hearts.   *1 John 5:21*

My child, listen and be wise. Keep your heart on the right course.   *Proverbs 23:19*

THE INTENT OF A GUARDRAIL on a dangerous curve is not to inhibit your freedom to drive but to save your life! That guardrail is a sign of security and safety, not an obstacle to driving. In the same way, you need a guardrail as you travel through life, not to inhibit your freedom but to keep your life from going out of control. Your heart determines where you go because it most affects your passions and emotions. If you don't guard your heart with God's Word and stay focused on the road God has put you on, you may have a terrible accident when temptation distracts you.

GOD'S CHALLENGE

These were his instructions to them: "You must always act in the fear of the LORD, with integrity and with undivided hearts."   *2 Chronicles 19:9*

　　　　　　　　　　　TRUST

Can I trust God enough to give him my whole heart? Can I let him love me?

GOD'S RESPONSE

All heaven will praise your miracles, LORD; myriads of angels will praise you for your faithfulness.　*Psalm 89:5*

I will be faithful to you and make you mine, and you will finally know me as LORD.　*Hosea 2:20*

He is the faithful God who keeps his covenant for a thousand generations.　*Deuteronomy 7:9*

WHEN YOU FALL IN LOVE, you make a series of decisions to trust the woman more and more as you get to know her. As you get to know God, you will find him more and more trustworthy. Unlike human relationships in which even the strongest love can sometimes fail you, God's love is perfect and will never let you down. Over time, if you keep deciding to trust God, you will develop complete confidence to trust him with all areas of your life.

GOD'S PROMISE

Nothing in all creation will ever be able to separate us from the love of God.　*Romans 8:39*

HEARTBREAK

I've been deeply hurt. How do I recover from a broken heart?

GOD'S RESPONSE

From the ends of the earth, I will cry to you for help, for my heart is overwhelmed. Lead me to the towering rock of safety. *Psalm 61:2*

The LORD hears the cries of his needy ones; he does not despise his people who are oppressed. *Psalm 69:33*

Great is his faithfulness; his mercies begin afresh each day. *Lamentations 3:23*

THERE IS NO QUICK ANTIDOTE for a broken heart. No pill, taken twice a day for two weeks, will cure it. Only God is the Master Healer; others can help, but no one can touch your broken heart and heal it as he can. When you are hurting, move toward God and not away from him, for he is the great source of joy and healing. His mercy is fresh every morning.

GOD'S PROMISE

Our hearts ache, but we always have joy. We are poor, but we give spiritual riches to others. We own nothing, and yet we have everything. *2 Corinthians 6:10*

GOD'S LOVE

How much does God love me?

GOD'S RESPONSE

His unfailing love toward those who fear him is as great as the height of the heavens above the earth.   *Psalm 103:11*

Your unfailing love is as high as the heavens. Your faithfulness reaches to the clouds.   *Psalm 57:10*

Long ago the LORD said to Israel: "I have loved you, my people, with an everlasting love. With unfailing love I have drawn you to myself."   *Jeremiah 31:3*

GOD CREATED YOU, LOVES YOU, and longs to have a relationship with you. He pursues you with persistent and unfailing love, drawing you to himself. Today, ask God to open your spiritual eyes to see which events, conversations, "chance" meetings, thoughts, and open doors are God's hand reaching out to show you he is nearby and at work in your life.

GOD'S PROMISE

"The mountains may depart and the hills disappear, but even then I will remain loyal to you. My covenant of blessing will never be broken," says the LORD, who has mercy on you.   *Isaiah 54:10*

GOD'S LOVE

How does God show his love for me?

GOD'S RESPONSE

For the Son of Man came to seek and save those who are lost.   *Luke 19:10 (NLT2)*

The law was given through Moses; God's unfailing love and faithfulness came through Jesus Christ.   *John 1:17*

When I am lifted up on the cross, I will draw everyone to myself.   *John 12:32*

IF YOU LOSE SOMETHING PRECIOUS to you, you search everywhere until you find it. You never give up looking for it. Likewise, you are precious to God. He pursued you when you were lost in sinfulness, and he continues to pursue you whenever you wander from him. He shows his love for you every day by drawing you to himself.

GOD'S PROMISE

God showed how much he loved us by sending his only Son into the world so that we might have eternal life through him.   *1 John 4:9*

DEPENDENCE

*How can I know that God is always with me?
Should I be completely dependent on him?*

GOD'S RESPONSE

Be sure of this: I am with you always, even to the end of the age.   *Matthew 28:20*

I know the LORD is always with me. I will not be shaken, for he is right beside me.   *Psalm 16:8*

When you bow down before the Lord and admit your dependence on him, he will lift you up and give you honor.
James 4:10

YOU CAN NEVER BE ALONE when you believe in Jesus, for his Spirit is always with you. And there is no one more dependable than the one who created you and knows you better than anyone else does. One of the mysteries of the Christian faith is that the more you humble yourself and depend on God, the stronger you become in character and integrity. When you are completely dependent on God, you can rely completely on his strength.

GOD'S PROMISE

Do not be afraid, for I am with you.   *Isaiah 43:5*

RELATIONSHIP

Why does God desire a relationship with me?

GOD'S RESPONSE

For he loves us with unfailing love; the faithfulness of the LORD endures forever. Praise the LORD!   *Psalm 117:2*

You are a God of forgiveness, gracious and merciful, slow to become angry, and full of unfailing love and mercy. *Nehemiah 9:17*

See how very much our heavenly Father loves us, for he allows us to be called his children, and we really are! But the people who belong to this world don't know God, so they don't understand that we are his children.   *1 John 3:1*

JUST AS A FATHER DESIRES A RELATIONSHIP with his son, so God desires a relationship with you. He created you and is responsible for you; he loves you with a faithful and unfailing love that endures forever. Because of his love for you, you are accepted and called his child. Accept his love gratefully and love him in return.

GOD'S PROMISE

God loves you dearly, and he has called you to be his very own people.   *Romans 1:7*

LOVE

How can I know God really loves me?

GOD'S RESPONSE

For God so loved the world that he gave his only Son, so that everyone who believes in him will not perish but have eternal life.   *John 3:16*

This is real love. It is not that we loved God, but that he loved us and sent his Son as a sacrifice to take away our sins.   *1 John 4:10*

Can anything ever separate us from Christ's love?
Romans 8:35

Y OU CAN KNOW FOR CERTAIN of God's great love for you because he allowed his Son to die in your place, to take the punishment for your sin so that you can be free from eternal judgment. Think of it: He sent his Son to die for you so that you could live forever with him. No wonder John wrote, "This is real love."

GOD'S PROMISE

I will never fail you. I will never forsake you.
Hebrews 13:5

LOVE

How can I show my love for God?

GOD'S RESPONSE

If you love me, obey my commandments.   *John 14:15*

When you obey me, you remain in my love. . . . I have told you this so that you will be filled with my joy. Yes, your joy will overflow!   *John 15:10-11*

O people, the LORD has already told you what is good, and this is what he requires: to do what is right, to love mercy, and to walk humbly with your God.   *Micah 6:8*

I F YOU HAVE CHILDREN, you know that they usually try to obey because they want to please you, even if they don't always achieve it. That is what God desires from his children. He knows that because of our sinful nature, we won't always obey his Word. What he wants is our desire to obey, because that is the sign that we love and respect him, and believe that his way for us is best. If you consistently disobey because you enjoy it, that is not showing love. What can you do today to show God that you love him?

GOD'S PROMISE

If you will obey me and keep my covenant, you will be my own special treasure from among all the nations of the earth; for all the earth belongs to me.   *Exodus 19:5*

　　　　　　　　　# INTIMACY

How is it possible to have intimacy with God?

GOD'S RESPONSE

I will be with you, and I will protect you wherever you go. . . . I will be with you constantly until I have finished giving you everything I have promised.　　*Genesis 28:15*

T O SHARE INTIMACY means to be completely vulnerable to someone, to know fully and be fully known. Intimacy occurs in only the most personal relationships. We often resist being vulnerable to God about our sins, especially the ones we don't want to give up, but intimacy requires full disclosure, not hiding or covering up. When we admit and confess our sin, seek forgiveness, and commit ourselves to obeying God, our relationship with God is restored and we can know him in a truly intimate way. God is a personal being who created people for the purpose of intimacy with himself. When you respond and accept his love, he becomes closer than a brother or even a spouse.

GOD'S PROMISE

The LORD your God has arrived to live among you. . . . He will exult over you by singing a happy song. *Zephaniah 3:17*

INTIMACY

What does it mean to have intimacy with God?

GOD'S RESPONSE

The LORD replied, "I will personally go with you."
Exodus 33:14

The next morning Jesus awoke long before daybreak and went out alone into the wilderness to pray.   *Mark 1:35*

SOME PEOPLE WOULD HAVE US CHOOSE between quality time and quantity time. The intimacy of any relationship is a function of both the amount of time spent together and the quality of what is accomplished or shared in that time. If a husband and wife spend three hours a day together, but those hours are spent watching television, it is hard for them to establish intimacy. So it is in our relationship with God. An intimate relationship with God grows out of both the quantity and the quality of the time that we spend focused on him. Do you intentionally and consistently spend time alone with God?

GOD'S PROMISE

Surely your goodness and unfailing love will pursue me all the days of my life, and I will live in the house of the LORD forever.   *Psalm 23:6*

CONTENTMENT

How do I find true contentment in life?

GOD'S RESPONSE

"Brother, I have plenty," Esau answered. "Keep what you have." *Genesis 33:9*

Get rid of all bitterness. *Ephesians 4:31*

ESAU APPARENTLY LEARNED to be content with what he had rather than letting his feelings fester over what he had lost. But there was a time when he wanted to kill Jacob for his deceit (Genesis 27:41). Because life sometimes brings unpleasant circumstances our way, we will feel cheated, angry, and frustrated at times. These emotions are natural (especially to our sinful nature), but if we hold on to them they turn into bitterness. Bitterness and contentment cannot coexist. We can prevent bitterness by being honest with God about how we feel, by forgiving those who wrong us, and by concentrating on God's good gifts to us. Isn't it a much better choice to forgive and move on?

GOD'S CHALLENGE

To enjoy your work and accept your lot in life—that is indeed a gift from God. People who do this rarely look with sorrow on the past, for God has given them reasons for joy. *Ecclesiastes 5:19-20*

WORSHIP

What is worship, and why is it important?

GOD'S RESPONSE

We adore you as the one who is over all things. Riches and honor come from you alone, for you rule over everything. . . . Our God, we thank you and praise your glorious name!   *1 Chronicles 29:11-13*

H UMAN BEINGS IN EVERY TIME and culture have demonstrated a need and desire to worship someone more powerful than themselves. In the Bible, worship means recognizing the power and authority of God and offering praise, gifts, and obedience in response. Who or what do you worship? That is the most important question of human existence, for that determines your beliefs, values, and behavior. Do you give your allegiance and obedience to any "lesser gods," such as money, status, or people? The Bible teaches that only one God is truly worthy of our worship, for he alone is holy and sovereign, possessing the authority to judge all things.

GOD'S PROMISE

Who will not fear, O Lord, and glorify your name? For you alone are holy. All nations will come and worship before you, for your righteous deeds have been revealed. *Revelation 15:4*

PRESENCE

How can I enter God's presence?

GOD'S RESPONSE

Let us come before him with thanksgiving. Let us sing him psalms of praise.   *Psalm 95:2*

Worship the LORD with gladness. Come before him, singing with joy.   *Psalm 100:2*

Enter his gates with thanksgiving; go into his courts with praise. Give thanks to him and bless his name.
Psalm 100:4

I F YOU ARE A CHRISTIAN, you already are in God's presence, but if you need help in feeling God's presence, begin by worshiping him. Approach him with gladness, with a joyful song in your heart. Praise and thank him for what he has done for you. This will make you more aware of God around you in nature, in moments of peace, in acts of kindness, and in the strength that he provides to help you through tough times.

GOD'S PROMISE

Look! Here I stand at the door and knock. If you hear me calling and open the door, I will come in, and we will share a meal as friends.   *Revelation 3:20*

PRESENCE

What are some benefits of being in God's presence?

GOD'S RESPONSE

Now, the Lord is the Spirit, and wherever the Spirit of the Lord is, he gives freedom.   *2 Corinthians 3:17*

You will show me the way of life, granting me the joy of your presence and the pleasures of living with you forever.   *Psalm 16:11*

I command you—be strong and courageous! Do not be afraid or discouraged. For the LORD your God is with you wherever you go.   *Joshua 1:9*

WHEN YOU REMAIN IN GOD'S PRESENCE, you have freedom, joy, and courage to face whatever life brings your way. Do not be discouraged when challenges come—you always have help at your side. Be strong in the knowledge that God is with you.

GOD'S PROMISE

When you go through deep waters and great trouble, I will be with you. When you go through rivers of difficulty, you will not drown! When you walk through the fire of oppression, you will not be burned up; the flames will not consume you.   *Isaiah 43:2*

DISTANCE

What should I do when I feel that God is far away?

GOD'S RESPONSE

O LORD, why do you stand so far away? Why do you hide when I need you the most? . . . LORD, you know the hopes of the helpless. Surely you will listen to their cries and comfort them.   *Psalm 10:1, 17*

I can never escape from your spirit! I can never get away from your presence!   *Psalm 139:7*

WHEN GOD SEEMS FAR AWAY, it is often because you have moved away, not God. The good news is that just like the father in the parable of the Prodigal Son (Luke 15:11-32), God is eagerly awaiting your return. You can follow David's example in the Psalms and draw close to God in prayer.

GOD'S PROMISE

I will make an everlasting covenant with them, promising not to stop doing good for them. I will put a desire in their hearts to worship me, and they will never leave me.
Jeremiah 32:40

NEARNESS

I often feel alone when I face difficulties in my life. Where is God in those times?

GOD'S RESPONSE

When the traders came by, his brothers pulled Joseph out of the pit and sold him for twenty pieces of silver. . . . The LORD was with Joseph, giving him success in everything he did.   *Genesis 37:28; 39:3*

We are hunted down, but God never abandons us. We get knocked down, but we get up again and keep going. *2 Corinthians 4:9*

THOUGH YOU MAY NOT FEEL God's presence or be able to see him working, you can be sure that God is always with you. Many of the heroes of the Bible felt alone at some point, and you should not be surprised when this happens to you as well. It is often during the times when your faith is challenged that you grow the most. God has a plan for everything, even loneliness. If you keep watching, you will see his plan for you unfold.

GOD'S PROMISE

The LORD will not abandon his chosen people. *1 Samuel 12:22*

SUFFERING

Does suffering mean that God doesn't care about me or that he's punishing me?

GOD'S RESPONSE

He has not ignored the suffering of the needy. He has not turned and walked away. He has listened to their cries for help.   *Psalm 22:24*

You keep track of all my sorrows. You have collected all my tears in your bottle. You have recorded each one in your book.   *Psalm 56:8*

I T IS LIKELY THAT NO ONE has suffered more than God's own Son when he was crucified, yet no one doubts God's love for Jesus. In the same way, our suffering does not mean that God has ever left us or stopped loving us. Your suffering matters to God because you matter to God. He may not remove the suffering from you, but he has promised to help you get through it.

GOD'S PROMISE

Those who plant in tears will harvest with shouts of joy. They weep as they go to plant their seed, but they sing as they return with the harvest.   *Psalm 126:5-6*

DISTRESS

When I am in trouble, how do I talk to God and know that he will hear me?

GOD'S RESPONSE

In my distress I cried out to the Lord; yes, I prayed to my God for help. He heard me from his sanctuary; my cry reached his ears.　*Psalm 18:6*

The Lord hears his people when they call to him for help. He rescues them from all their troubles.　*Psalm 34:17*

YOU DON'T NEED SPECIAL WORDS to talk to God. You can simply talk to God as you would to a trusted friend. God understands your emotions—he made them—so don't worry about getting too emotional with God. Tell him your fears and worries, and claim his promise to rescue you from temptation and danger and to stay with you no matter what comes.

GOD'S PROMISE

When they call on me, I will answer; I will be with them in trouble. I will rescue them and honor them. *Psalm 91:15*

SUFFERING

Can any good come from my suffering?

GOD'S RESPONSE

We are confident that as you share in our sufferings, you will also share in the comfort God gives us. *2 Corinthians 1:7 (NLT2)*

Since I know it is all for Christ's good, I am quite content with my weaknesses and with insults, hardships, persecutions, and calamities. For when I am weak, then I am strong. *2 Corinthians 12:10*

SOMETIMES YOU SUFFER FROM FACING the consequences of your own sin. At other times, suffering occurs because of events outside your control. Regardless of the reasons behind it, your faith is tested when you are suffering. During the hard times, your character is stretched and you are actively learning and growing.

GOD'S CHALLENGE

We can rejoice, too, when we run into problems and trials, for we know that they are good for us—they help us learn to endure. And endurance develops strength of character. *Romans 5:3-4*

SUFFERING

If I know I'm suffering because of past sins,
has God forgiven me?

GOD'S RESPONSE

I assure you that any sin can be forgiven.   *Mark 3:28*

He forgives all my sins and heals all my diseases. . . . He
has not punished us for all our sins, nor does he deal with
us as we deserve.   *Psalm 103:3, 10*

If we confess our sins to him, he is faithful and just to
forgive us and to cleanse us from every wrong.   *1 John 1:9*

FORGIVENESS MEANS THAT GOD LOOKS at you as
though you had never sinned. If you honestly confess
your sins to God, you can be sure that he will forgive you.
However, God designed the world to follow natural laws.
When these laws are broken, there are consequences that
you may still have to endure. Try to do so with patience
and humility, since you can be sure that God has forgiven
you and no longer counts your sins against you.

GOD'S PROMISE

I—yes, I alone—am the one who blots out your sins
for my own sake and will never think of them again.
Isaiah 43:25

CONFESSION

What happens when I confess my sin?

GOD'S RESPONSE

I confessed all my sins to you and stopped trying to hide them. I said to myself, "I will confess my rebellion to the LORD." And you forgave me! All my guilt is gone. *Psalm 32:5*

So now there is no condemnation for those who belong to Christ Jesus. *Romans 8:1*

Restore to me again the joy of your salvation, and make me willing to obey you. *Psalm 51:12*

C ONFESSION IS THE ACT OF RECOGNIZING your sins before God so he can forgive them; it indicates your desire to change your ways. Sin separates you from a holy God and confession brings you back into relationship with him. When you confess your sin, you agree that something wrong needs to be made right and that a damaged relationship with God needs to be restored.

GOD'S PROMISE

This is my blood, which seals the covenant between God and his people. It is poured out to forgive the sins of many. *Matthew 26:28*

FORGIVENESS

How does forgiveness make a difference in my life?

GOD'S RESPONSE

If you forgive those who sin against you, your heavenly Father will forgive you. But if you refuse to forgive others, your Father will not forgive your sins.   *Matthew 6:14-15*

Peter came to him and asked, "Lord, how often should I forgive someone who sins against me? Seven times?"
    "No!" Jesus replied, "seventy times seven!"
Matthew 18:21-22

FORGIVENESS IS A PATHWAY TO FREEDOM. When God forgives you, you are free from guilt and restored to fellowship with him. When you forgive someone who has wronged you, you are free from the bitterness and resentment that can settle in your heart. Receiving God's forgiveness and forgiving others are at the core of what it means to be a Christian. In doing this, we follow the example of God, who extends to us the ultimate pardon—forgiveness of our sins.

GOD'S CHALLENGE

You must make allowance for each other's faults and forgive the person who offends you. Remember, the Lord forgave you, so you must forgive others.   *Colossians 3:13*

FORGIVENESS

Is there a limit to how much God will forgive me?

GOD'S RESPONSE

All their past sins will be forgotten, and they will live because of the righteous things they have done. *Ezekiel 18:22*

With my authority, take this message of repentance to all the nations, beginning in Jerusalem: "There is forgiveness of sins for all who turn to me." *Luke 24:47*

He is so rich in kindness that he purchased our freedom through the blood of his Son, and our sins are forgiven. *Ephesians 1:7*

N O MATTER HOW TERRIBLE YOUR PAST, or how many sins you have committed, if you approach God with an attitude of humble sincerity and confess your sins, he will forgive you. To think that some of your sins are "too bad" to be forgiven is to minimize the power of Jesus' death and resurrection on your behalf.

GOD'S PROMISE

God has purchased our freedom with his blood and has forgiven all our sins. *Colossians 1:14*

FAILURE

How do I learn from failure and move on?

GOD'S RESPONSE

My dear children, I am writing this to you so that you will not sin. But if you do sin, there is someone to plead for you before the Father. He is Jesus Christ, the one who pleases God completely. He is the sacrifice for our sins. He takes away not only our sins but the sins of all the world.   *1 John 2:1-2*

They may trip seven times, but each time they will rise again.   *Proverbs 24:16*

YOUR FAILURE DOESN'T SURPRISE GOD. No matter how many times you fail, you can trust God to help you move forward. The best response to failure is to get up again and ask God what lesson you need to learn from that painful situation. Don't lose hope in the God who promises you ultimate victory through eternal life.

GOD'S PROMISE

Though I fall, I will rise again. Though I sit in darkness, the LORD himself will be my light.   *Micah 7:8*

FAILURE

*Everyone else seems to have perfect lives;
am I the only one who fails?*

GOD'S RESPONSE

Abraham told people there that his wife, Sarah, was his sister.   *Genesis 20:2*

Moses was badly frightened because he realized that everyone knew what he had done.   *Exodus 2:14*

David confessed to Nathan, "I have sinned against the LORD."   *2 Samuel 12:13*

Peter said, "Man, I don't know what you are talking about."   *Luke 22:60*

NO ONE IS EXEMPT FROM FAILING. Even heroes of the Bible such as Abraham, Moses, David, and Peter had firsthand experiences with failure. Jesus was the only man on earth who ever led a truly perfect life, but he was God! Fortunately, failure is not fatal. It does not mean you are substandard—only human. What you learn from your failure is what really counts.

GOD'S PROMISE

I cried out, "I'm slipping!" and your unfailing love, O LORD, supported me.   *Psalm 94:18*

SUCCESS

How can I turn my failure into success?

GOD'S RESPONSE

Be strong and courageous, and do the work. Don't be afraid or discouraged by the size of the task, for the Lord God, my God, is with you. He will not fail you or forsake you. He will see to it that all the work . . . is finished correctly.   *1 Chronicles 28:20*

DON'T BE AFRAID OF FAILING AGAIN. The only true failure is that which utterly defeats you and makes you unable to try again. Failure wins when you accept defeat and give up. Joshua was defeated at the battle of Ai. He dealt with the causes of defeat head-on, then led his army out once again into the danger of battle, and that time won a great victory. You must have the courage to face failure and take risks again. The lessons you learn from your failures will make you better able to handle similar situations in the future. If you don't give up, yesterday's failure will turn into tomorrow's victory.

GOD'S PROMISE

People who cover over their sins will not prosper. But if they confess and forsake them, they will receive mercy. *Proverbs 28:13*

SUCCESS

What is true success in God's eyes?

GOD'S RESPONSE

Study this Book of the Law continually. Meditate on it day and night so you may be sure to obey all that is written in it. Only then will you succeed.   *Joshua 1:8*

I intend to obey the commands of my God.
Psalm 119:115

Observe the requirements of the LORD your God and follow all his ways.   *1 Kings 2:3*

TRUE SUCCESS IS OBEYING GOD'S WORD, for it shows you God's will for your life and leads you to accomplish the job for which he created you. God's Word teaches you the truth and equips you with the skills and understanding to be productive, balanced, and wise.

GOD'S PROMISE

Commit your work to the LORD, and then your plans will succeed.   *Proverbs 16:3*

SUCCESS

What are the dangers of living for worldly success?

GOD'S RESPONSE

He gave an illustration: "A rich man had a fertile farm that produced fine crops. In fact, his barns were full to overflowing. So he said, 'I know! I'll tear down my barns and build bigger ones. Then I'll have room enough to store everything. And I'll sit back and say to myself, My friend, you have enough stored away for years to come. Now take it easy! Eat, drink, and be merry!' But God said to him, 'You fool! You will die this very night. Then who will get it all?' Yes, a person is a fool to store up earthly wealth but not have a rich relationship with God." *Luke 12:16-21*

HOW DANGEROUS IT IS to be a success in the world but a failure with God! To gain the world and lose your soul is the ultimate failure, for only your soul is eternal. It takes a truly wise investor to learn how to invest now in order to gain wealth and success in eternity.

GOD'S CHALLENGE

How do you benefit if you gain the whole world but lose or forfeit your own soul in the process? *Luke 9:25*

BLESSINGS

Is it okay to try to become wealthy?

GOD'S RESPONSE

The LORD was with Joseph and blessed him greatly . . . giving him success in everything he did.   *Genesis 39:2-3*

The LORD blessed Job in the second half of his life even more than in the beginning. . . . Job lived 140 years after that, living to see four generations of his children and grandchildren. Then he died, an old man who had lived a long, good life.   *Job 42:12, 16-17*

THE BIBLE MENTIONS MANY RICH PEOPLE who loved God without saying anything negative about their wealth (e.g., Abraham, David, Joseph of Arimathea, Lydia). Scripture doesn't focus on how much money you have, but rather on what you do with it. Jesus said, "Wherever your treasure is, there your heart and thoughts will also be" (Matthew 6:21). So work hard and succeed without guilt, but work just as hard to find ways of pleasing God with your generosity.

GOD'S CHALLENGE

God has given gifts to each of you. . . . Manage them well so that God's generosity can flow through you.
1 Peter 4:10

HIDING

Can I get away with sin?

GOD'S RESPONSE

Jacob called together all his sons and said, "Gather around me, and I will tell you what is going to happen to you in the days to come. . . . Reuben, you are my firstborn . . . but you are as unruly as a flood, and you will be first no longer. For you went to bed with my wife; you defiled my marriage couch. *Genesis 49:1, 3-4 (NLT2)*

I F YOU DO SOMETHING WRONG and no one finds out, or no one gets hurt, is it really wrong? Did you get away with it? Reuben might have thought he got away with sleeping with his father's concubine. No more was mentioned of Reuben's sin until Jacob mentioned it on his deathbed and took away Reuben's double portion of the family inheritance. Sin is wrong whether or not another person notices, and God always knows what we do. The consequences of our sin may not always be immediate, but they are inevitable.

GOD'S CHALLENGE

For the time is coming when everything that is covered will be revealed, and all that is secret will be made known to all. *Matthew 10:26 (NLT2)*

AMBITION

When is ambition good?

GOD'S RESPONSE

Happy are people of integrity, who follow the law of the LORD. Happy are those who . . . search for him with all their hearts.   *Psalm 119:1-2*

My ambition has always been to preach the Good News where the name of Christ has never been heard. *Romans 15:20*

A MBITION IS GOOD WHEN IT IS DIRECTED not at the size of an accomplishment but at the quality of your character. The best kind of ambition is to know God's will and then use your energies to pursue it. Paul's great ambition was to preach about Christ around the world. What great ambition has God laid on your heart?

GOD'S CHALLENGE

Make the most of every opportunity.   *Colossians 4:5*

AMBITION

When is ambition harmful?

GOD'S RESPONSE

Let's build a great city with a tower that reaches to the skies—a monument to our greatness!   *Genesis 11:4*

How terrible it will be for you who get rich by unjust means! . . . How terrible it will be for you who build cities with money gained by murder and corruption! *Habakkuk 2:9, 12*

You want what you don't have, so you scheme and kill to get it. You are jealous for what others have, and you can't possess it, so you fight and quarrel to take it away from them.   *James 4:2*

THERE'S A DIFFERENCE between being a part of God's great work and wanting personal greatness through God's work. If you're not sure where you fall, examine your motives. If the greatest benefactor of your achievements is yourself, then perhaps your ambition is out of control. Seek to honor God and others, not yourself.

GOD'S CHALLENGE

Jesus said to the disciples, "If any of you wants to be my follower, you must put aside your selfish ambition, shoulder your cross, and follow me."   *Matthew 16:24*

AMBITION

How do I guard against selfish ambition?

GOD'S RESPONSE

Everything else is worthless when compared with the priceless gain of knowing Christ Jesus my Lord. *Philippians 3:8*

May he give us the desire to do his will in everything and to obey all the commands, laws, and regulations that he gave our ancestors.   *1 Kings 8:58*

SELFISH AMBITION FADES as your ambition to serve God grows. No earthly achievement can compare to the ultimate accomplishment of having lived this life with a great love for the Lord and a desire to serve him. This brings you the greatest reward of all—eternal life with him—as well as many other enduring rewards. In fact, you must be careful that your earthly achievements don't distract and prevent you from loving God, or you will forfeit the greatest promotion you'll ever have! Put your energy into something that will last forever.

GOD'S PROMISE

Happy are people of integrity, who follow the law of the LORD. Happy are those who . . . search for him with all their hearts.   *Psalm 119:1-2*

LEADERSHIP

What are some qualities of a godly leader?

GOD'S RESPONSE

Whoever wants to be a leader among you must be your servant.   *Matthew 20:26*

An elder must be a man whose life cannot be spoken against.   *1 Timothy 3:2*

GODLY LEADERS DEMONSTRATE MATURITY, both in their actions and in their knowledge of God's Word. They are more interested in serving than in being served. They are more humble than proud, and they do not call attention to their own accomplishments. Their lifestyle cannot be criticized. They do not teach things that contradict the Scripture. Their goal is to unite people, not divide them. They love to talk about spiritual things and the evidence of Jesus in their life. They are known for their close walk with God. If you are in some leadership capacity, how well do your leadership qualities match this list?

GOD'S PROMISE

I will give you leaders after my own heart, who will guide you with knowledge and understanding.   *Jeremiah 3:15*

LEADERSHIP

What are some keys to effective leadership?

GOD'S RESPONSE

The LORD told Abram, "Leave your country, your relatives, and your father's house, and go to the land that I will show you." . . . Abram departed as the LORD had instructed him. *Genesis 12:1, 4*

How can I settle all your quarrels and problems by myself? Choose some men from each tribe who have wisdom, understanding, and a good reputation, and I will appoint them as your leaders. *Deuteronomy 1:12-13*

I pressed further, "What you are doing is not right!" *Nehemiah 5:9*

EFFECTIVE LEADERS SEEK GOD'S CALL for their lives, settle quarrels, deal with problems, delegate responsibilities to trustworthy subordinates, and courageously stand up to those who are doing wrong. Their mission is to keep peace among the people in their circle of influence.

GOD'S CHALLENGE

You didn't choose me. I chose you. I appointed you to go and produce fruit that will last. *John 15:16*

INSPIRATION

As a leader, how can I inspire hope?

GOD'S RESPONSE

Perhaps you will think to yourselves, "How can we ever conquer these nations that are so much more powerful than we are?" But don't be afraid of them! Just remember what the LORD your God did to Pharaoh and to all the land of Egypt.   *Deuteronomy 7:17-18*

You will enjoy a long life in the land the LORD swore to give to your ancestors and to you, their descendants— a land flowing with milk and honey!   *Deuteronomy 11:9*

YOU INSPIRE HOPE IN OTHERS by reminding them of God's past blessings, by presenting them with a positive vision of the future, and by speaking and acting in ways that show your complete confidence in the Lord's provision. By remembering together how God has delivered you in the past, you remind others of the blessings awaiting you in the future.

GOD'S CHALLENGE

Be strong and take courage, all you who put your hope in the LORD!   *Psalm 31:24*

CHALLENGES

What do I need to know about challenges and risks?

GOD'S RESPONSE

A prudent person foresees the danger ahead and takes precautions; the simpleton goes blindly on and suffers the consequences.   *Proverbs 22:3*

Can anything ever separate us from Christ's love? Does it mean he no longer loves us if we have trouble or calamity, or are persecuted, or are hungry or cold or in danger or threatened with death?   *Romans 8:35*

THE BIBLE SAYS MANY THINGS about risks and challenges. For example: risk is part of life; smart people try to assess and plan for risk before jumping in; risks and challenges can help you grow in character because you have to work hard to overcome obstacles while relying on the Lord; and no matter what the risk or what the challenge, nothing can separate you from God's love.

GOD'S CHALLENGE

Do not be afraid of the terrors of the night, nor fear the dangers of the day, nor dread the plague that stalks in darkness, nor the disaster that strikes at midday. *Psalm 91:5-6*

CHANGE

Is change necessary?

GOD'S RESPONSE

Jewish believers who came with Peter were amazed that the gift of the Holy Spirit had been poured out upon the Gentiles, too. And there could be no doubt about it. *Acts 10:45-46*

You have clothed yourselves with a brand-new nature that is continually being renewed as you learn more and more about Christ, who created this new nature within you. *Colossians 3:10*

G OD IS IN THE BUSINESS of changing lives. We are always changing in response to his call and becoming more like him. Leaders are, by definition, also in the business of change. Whether by helping others change raw materials into finished products, changing people from uneducated to educated, or leading others through political and social change, a good leader understands the necessity of change and the tensions involved. Change is a constant in life, but the question is: Are you changing for better or for worse?

GOD'S PROMISE

Create in me a clean heart, O God. Renew a right spirit within me.   *Psalm 51:10*

CHARACTER

Does a leader's character matter?

GOD'S RESPONSE

Suppose a certain man . . . stays away from injustice, is honest and fair when judging others, and faithfully obeys my laws and regulations. Anyone who does these things is just and will surely live, says the Sovereign LORD. *Ezekiel 18:5, 8-9*

Even children are known by the way they act, whether their conduct is pure and right.   *Proverbs 20:11*

I F A LEADER PERFORMS WELL in his public life, does his personal life matter? Yes. Justice, righteousness, integrity, mercy, honesty, fairness, and faithfulness are essential traits because they reflect who a person really is. For example, you cannot be honest in your public life and be a liar and cheat in your personal life. It doesn't work that way. You are who you are, twenty-four hours a day. If you are demonstrating ungodly characteristics, you can be sure they will surface in all areas of your life—personal and public.

GOD'S CHALLENGE

Unless you are faithful in small matters, you won't be faithful in large ones. If you cheat even a little, you won't be honest with greater responsibilities.   *Luke 16:10*

DECISIONS

How can I make good decisions as a leader?

GOD'S RESPONSE

Trust in the LORD with all your heart; do not depend on your own understanding. Seek his will in all you do, and he will direct your paths.   *Proverbs 3:5-6*

Rehoboam rejected the advice of the elders and instead asked the opinion of the young men who had grown up with him and who were now his advisers.   *1 Kings 12:8*

Intelligent people are always open to new ideas. In fact, they look for them.   *Proverbs 18:15*

BEGIN ALL DECISIONS WITH HUMILITY and reverence for God, because you are ultimately accountable to him. Be careful when seeking advice from others. Weigh their advice carefully and you will be more likely to make good choices. Being open to good advice and seeking godly counsel is not a sign of weakness or inadequacy, but of wisdom.

GOD'S PROMISE

Your decrees please me; they give me wise advice.
Psalm 119:24

EXAMPLE

As a leader, what can I learn from Jesus' example?

GOD'S RESPONSE

You have heard that the law of Moses says . . . but I say . . .
Matthew 5:21-22

Jesus said to the people who believed in him, "You are truly my disciples if you keep obeying my teachings. And you will know the truth, and the truth will set you free."
John 8:31-32

PART OF A LEADER'S RESPONSIBILITY is to help those they lead to develop a worldview and perspective of God's truth that enables them to interpret life from an eternal point of view. The truth, even when it is hard, sets people free from ignorance and deception. As a leader, it is your responsibility to keep God's truth at the center of all you do and of every decision you make. Then you will be doing the right thing—that which is wise and approved of by God. This applies whether you are the leader of a family, a church group, or a large corporation.

GOD'S PROMISE

He replied, "What is impossible from a human perspective is possible with God."   *Luke 18:27*

DELEGATION

What is good about sharing responsibility?

GOD'S RESPONSE

This job is too heavy a burden for you to handle all by yourself. *Exodus 18:18*

He called his twelve disciples together and sent them out two by two. *Mark 6:7*

MOSES WAS AN ENORMOUSLY GIFTED LEADER who fell into the trap of believing he had to do it all by himself. It is possible to be too responsible. When you stretch yourself too thin you put yourself and others at risk. You can wear yourself out, make others wait, prevent those with gifts from having the opportunity to use them, and keep them from growing spiritually through serving others. In the process, God's people become dissatisfied and distracted and God's work is delayed. Jethro's advice to Moses in the book of Exodus has been God's strategy from the beginning: delegation and discipleship.

GOD'S CHALLENGE

Go and make disciples of all the nations, baptizing them in the name of the Father and the Son and the Holy Spirit. Teach these new disciples to obey all the commands I have given you. *Matthew 28:19-20*

EXAMPLE

How do I set an example when I lead others?

GOD'S RESPONSE

You should follow my example, just as I follow Christ's.
1 Corinthians 11:1

You yourself must be an example to them by doing good
deeds of every kind.   *Titus 2:7*

For even I, the Son of Man, came here not to be served
but to serve others.   *Matthew 20:28*

S OMETIMES, LEADERS ARE TEMPTED to think that they
are special and thus exempt from the standards that
apply to everyone else. A good leader abides by the same
rules as his followers and practices what he preaches.
Resist the temptation to think that your authority makes
you the exception. Work as hard as the rest, or harder.
When your life is consistent with the standards you expect
of others, you will set a good example as a leader.

GOD'S CHALLENGE

He did what was pleasing in the Lord's sight and
followed the example of his ancestor David. He did not
turn aside from doing what was right.   *2 Kings 22:2*

RATIONALIZATION

What is the danger of rationalization?

GOD'S RESPONSE

Judah said to the others, "What can we gain by killing our brother? That would just give us a guilty conscience. Let's sell Joseph to those Ishmaelite traders. Let's not be responsible for his death; after all, he is our brother!"
Genesis 37:26-27

JOSEPH'S BROTHERS ALTERED their initial plan of killing Joseph to just selling him into slavery. Rationalization of a lesser sin does not change sin from being sin. When you find yourself rationalizing your actions, it's time to pause and truthfully assess your motives and their potential consequences. Rationalizing is trying to convince yourself that wrong is right, that sin isn't so bad if it is a lesser sin. It is convincing yourself that your choices have no consequences. Watch today for where you may be rationalizing your actions rather than standing up for what is right.

GOD'S CHALLENGE

Be careful how you live among your unbelieving neighbors. Even if they accuse you of doing wrong, they will see your honorable behavior, and they will believe and give honor to God when he comes to judge the world.   *1 Peter 2:12*

MOTIVATION

How can I motivate those I lead?

GOD'S RESPONSE

Someone said to Jesus, "I will follow you no matter where you go."

But Jesus replied, "Foxes have dens to live in, and birds have nests, but I, the Son of Man, have no home of my own, not even a place to lay my head." . . .

Another said, "Yes, Lord, I will follow you, but first let me say good-bye to my family."

But Jesus told him, "Anyone who puts a hand to the plow and then looks back is not fit for the Kingdom of God." *Luke 9:57-58, 61-62*

G OOD LEADERS LET PEOPLE KNOW what they expect of them. Set a goal that is challenging but achievable and explain how you will determine when the goal is met. Like Jesus, explain the costs and rewards of following. If you don't believe in what you are doing, neither will those who follow you.

GOD'S PROMISE

If you try to keep your life for yourself, you will lose it. But if you give up your life for me, you will find true life. *Luke 9:24*

SERVANT LEADERSHIP

What does it mean to be a servant leader?

GOD'S RESPONSE

He got up from the table, took off his robe, wrapped a towel around his waist, and poured water into a basin. Then he began to wash the disciples' feet and to wipe them with the towel he had around him.   *John 13:4-5*

Whoever wants to be a leader among you must be your servant.   *Matthew 20:26*

JESUS REVOLUTIONIZED LEADERSHIP. In a striking picture of servanthood, Jesus humbled himself by performing the task of a slave, showing how far we are to go in serving others. As a servant leader, you should be willing to perform any task you delegate to others. How can you demonstrate servant leadership today at home, work, church, or with your neighbor?

GOD'S CHALLENGE

Since I, the Lord and Teacher, have washed your feet, you ought to wash each other's feet. I have given you an example to follow. Do as I have done to you.
John 13:14-15

SUBSTITUTION

Why did Jesus die on the cross?

GOD'S RESPONSE

No one can take my life from me. I lay down my life voluntarily. For I have the right to lay it down when I want to and also the power to take it again. For my Father has given me this command.   *John 10:18*

You know that God paid a ransom to save you from the empty life you inherited from your ancestors. . . . He paid for you with the precious lifeblood of Christ, the sinless, spotless Lamb of God.   *1 Peter 1:18-19*

I F THE PRESIDENT OF THE UNITED STATES offered to be executed in the place of a convicted criminal, we would be amazed. How much more should we be amazed that the God of the universe took our place, accepting the punishment we deserved for our sin. His willingness to make the ultimate sacrifice for you demonstrates his great love for you.

GOD'S PROMISE

The gatekeeper opens the gate for him, and the sheep hear his voice and come to him. He calls his own sheep by name and leads them out.   *John 10:3*

REMEMBRANCE

How can remembering God help my spiritual walk?

GOD'S RESPONSE

You must commit yourselves wholeheartedly to these commands I am giving you today. Repeat them again and again to your children. . . . Write them on the doorposts of your house and on your gates.   *Deuteronomy 6:6-7, 9*

MOSES REMINDED THE PEOPLE to take every opportunity of every day to remember God's Word and to tell family and friends of God's past help and blessings. If you do this each day you will strengthen your love and commitment to God, and this will motivate you to be even more faithful in the following days. God helps you to fight and to win life's battles. Remember God the first thing in the morning and as you fall asleep at night. Remember God as the source of the hope you think you've lost. Remember God with a thankful heart when you have plenty, for you will need him when you have little. Weave him into the fabric of your life and your spiritual walk will be strong and focused.

GOD'S PROMISE

If you keep looking steadily into God's perfect law—the law that sets you free—and if you do what it says and don't forget what you heard, then God will bless you for doing it.   *James 1:25*

CROSS

What does the Cross mean for my life today?

GOD'S RESPONSE

He gave his life to free us from every kind of sin, to cleanse us, and to make us his very own people, totally committed to doing what is right.   *Titus 2:14*

Put aside your selfish ambition, shoulder your cross, and follow me. . . . If you give up your life for my sake and for the sake of the Good News, you will find true life. *Mark 8:34-35*

W HEN YOU ARE ABSOLUTELY CONVINCED that Jesus died on the cross to spare you from eternal punishment and to give you the free gift of eternal life, then the troubles of this world are put in perspective. You know that your future—for all eternity—is secure. This gives you peace no matter what happens in this life and changes the way you react to the difficulties life throws your way. Your sinful nature no longer controls you; you are free to live as God wants you to live.

GOD'S PROMISE

Those who belong to Christ Jesus have nailed the passions and desires of their sinful nature to his cross and crucified them there.   *Galatians 5:24*

DEATH

What happens after I die?

GOD'S RESPONSE

We will each receive whatever we deserve for the good or evil we have done in our bodies.   *2 Corinthians 5:10*

There are many rooms in my Father's home, and I am going to prepare a place for you.   *John 14:2*

WHAT HAPPENS AFTER YOU DIE depends on whether you believe that Jesus is who he said he is. If you believe that Jesus is the Son of God who died for your sins, and if you let him forgive your sins and allow him control of your life, he guarantees that you will live forever in heaven. When you travel, it's comforting to know that there is a place to stay at the end of the day. This same comfort is yours as you think of your life journey—you will end up in heaven. What happens after you die is the most important issue you must consider. If you don't want death to be the end of life with God, you must live as though eternal life with Jesus is already beginning.

GOD'S PROMISE

I am the resurrection and the life. Those who believe in me, even though they die like everyone else, will live again.   *John 11:25*

RESURRECTION

What does Jesus' resurrection mean to me?

GOD'S RESPONSE

For God so loved the world that he gave his only Son, so that everyone who believes in him will not perish but have eternal life.   *John 3:16*

Our earthly bodies, which die and decay, will be different when they are resurrected, for they will never die. *1 Corinthians 15:42*

W ITHOUT THE RESURRECTION of Jesus from the dead there would be no Christianity. The Resurrection demonstrates God's power over death and gives us the assurance that we also will be resurrected. The power of God that brought Jesus back from the dead can bring you back to life if you have asked him to forgive your sins and give you a new life in him. Jesus' death was not the end. Instead, his resurrection was the beginning of eternal life for all who believe in him.

GOD'S PROMISE

I am going to prepare a place for you. If this were not so, I would tell you plainly. When everything is ready, I will come and get you, so that you will always be with me where I am.   *John 14:2-3*

NEWNESS

What will my body be like after it is resurrected?

GOD'S RESPONSE

Then God gives it a new body—just the kind he wants it to have.   *1 Corinthians 15:38*

Our bodies now disappoint us, but when they are raised, they will be full of glory. They are weak now, but when they are raised, they will be full of power. They are natural human bodies now, but when they are raised, they will be spiritual bodies. For just as there are natural bodies, so also there are spiritual bodies.   *1 Corinthians 15:43-44*

YOUR RESURRECTED BODY will be a literal and physical body like you have now, except that it will also have many supernatural characteristics. You may be able to walk through walls, as Jesus did with his resurrected body. More importantly, your new body won't ever decay from the effects of sin. You will never be sick or in pain again, nor will your mind think sinful thoughts. You will be fully and finally perfect in God's sight.

GOD'S PROMISE

We will not all die, but we will all be transformed! . . . Our mortal bodies must be transformed into immortal bodies.   *1 Corinthians 15:51, 53 (NLT2)*

CONFIDENCE

How can I have confidence that God will someday resurrect me?

GOD'S RESPONSE

As to whether there will be a resurrection of the dead . . . long after Abraham, Isaac, and Jacob had died, God said, "I am the God of Abraham, the God of Isaac, and the God of Jacob." So he is the God of the living, not the dead. *Matthew 22:31-32*

YOU CAN ONLY BE CONFIDENT that you will be raised from the dead if you believe that Jesus died for your sins—that he was truly dead and that he rose from the dead and ascended into heaven. If Jesus was raised from the dead with a new body, then he was who God claimed he was, for no human has ever had power over death. And if Jesus is God, you can believe him when he says that those who believe in him are assured of also being resurrected and of living forever with him in heaven. Do you believe? Your very life depends on it.

GOD'S PROMISE

I am the resurrection and the life. Those who believe in me, even though they die like everyone else, will live again. *John 11:25*

FOOLISHNESS

How does the Bible define fools and foolishness?

GOD'S RESPONSE

Only fools say in their hearts, "There is no God."
Psalm 14:1

Fear of the LORD is the beginning of knowledge. Only fools despise wisdom and discipline.   *Proverbs 1:7*

Anyone who hears my teaching and ignores it is foolish, like a person who builds a house on sand. When the rains and floods come and the winds beat against that house, it will fall with a mighty crash.   *Matthew 7:26-27*

THE BIBLE DESCRIBES A FOOL as a person who refuses to acknowledge God's existence; makes no attempt to develop wisdom and self-discipline; enjoys making fun of that which is good and moral; speaks carelessly and thoughtlessly about others; and thinks he or she is always right. Let "April Fools" describe the day, and not you!

GOD'S CHALLENGE

Those who bring trouble on their families inherit only the wind. The fool will be a servant to the wise.
Proverbs 11:29

FOOLISHNESS

How can I keep from acting foolishly?

GOD'S RESPONSE

As a dog returns to its vomit, so a fool repeats his folly.
Proverbs 26:11

A person is a fool to store up earthly wealth but not have a rich relationship with God. *Luke 12:21*

Stop fooling yourselves. If you think you are wise by this world's standards, you will have to become a fool so you can become wise by God's standards. For the wisdom of this world is foolishness to God. *1 Corinthians 3:18-19*

THERE'S NOTHING WRONG with enjoying life on this earth unless it is at the expense of a relationship with God, or in violation of the standards of living written in his Word. Hundreds of wise sayings are found in the Bible to keep you from doing stupid things. Neglecting the basic truths of God's wisdom is the greatest act of foolishness.

GOD'S CHALLENGE

The wise inherit honor, but fools are put to shame!
Proverbs 3:35

ACCOUNTABILITY

*How does accountability help me avoid
foolish mistakes?*

GOD'S RESPONSE

Fools think they need no advice, but the wise listen to
others.   *Proverbs 12:15*

THERE ARE PROBABLY some dark corners in your life—
secret habits and private thoughts that you don't
want anyone to know about. If those were exposed to
the spotlight of God's truth, you know you would have
to deal with them, even give them up. Accountability
means answering to someone who will ask you to give an
account of your words, actions, and motives—even the
ones in dark corners. Accountability can be painful in the
short run, but the lack of it will destroy you in the long
run. Your secret sins will eat away at your character and
integrity until your reputation crashes around you. Rarely
do you see it coming. Determine now to find a wise friend
or mentor to keep you accountable. Don't let the darkness
take over your heart.

GOD'S CHALLENGE

Share each other's troubles and problems, and in this way
obey the law of Christ.   *Galatians 6:2*

CONFRONTATION

How can I effectively confront someone who is heading toward foolishness?

GOD'S RESPONSE

Take no part in the worthless deeds of evil and darkness; instead, rebuke and expose them.   *Ephesians 5:11*

If another believer sins, rebuke him; then if he repents, forgive him.   *Luke 17:3*

They must not speak evil of anyone, and they must avoid quarreling. Instead, they should be gentle and show true humility to everyone.   *Titus 3:2*

HOW YOU CONFRONT SOMEONE is just as important as what you say. Effective confrontation is first done privately, gently, and with pure motives. If you are convinced that confrontation is necessary, it is best to approach the person sooner rather than later. The person may be upset at first, so be kind and patient. Remember that it is God who changes hearts, not you. Consider how you would want to be confronted—and then take your own advice!

GOD'S CHALLENGE

If you punish a mocker, the simpleminded will learn a lesson; if you reprove the wise, they will be all the wiser. *Proverbs 19:25*

CONFRONTATION

How should I respond when I am confronted?

GOD'S RESPONSE

They confronted King Uzziah and said, "It is not for you, Uzziah, to burn incense to the LORD." . . . Uzziah was furious and refused to set down the incense burner he was holding. But as he was standing there with the priests before the incense altar in the LORD's Temple, leprosy suddenly broke out on his forehead.   *2 Chronicles 26:18-19*

I recognize my shameful deeds—they haunt me day and night. . . . Purify me from my sins, and I will be clean; wash me, and I will be whiter than snow.   *Psalm 51:3, 7*

K ING UZZIAH WAS FURIOUS when rightly confronted for his wrongdoing. He refused to change, and he suffered the consequences. On the other hand, the humility in King David's response to confrontation—admitting his wrongdoing and asking for forgiveness—provides a great model. When confronted, you should be honored that someone cares enough about you to want what is best for you and that they are willing to risk your anger in order to speak the truth.

GOD'S CHALLENGE

An open rebuke is better than hidden love!   *Proverbs 27:5*

RESPONSIBILITY

How can I do the right things more often?

GOD'S RESPONSE

It was the woman you gave me who brought me the fruit, and I ate it.   *Genesis 3:12*

[Pilate] sent for a bowl of water and washed his hands before the crowd, saying, "I am innocent of the blood of this man. The responsibility is yours!"   *Matthew 27:24*

Don't try to avoid responsibility by saying you didn't know about it. For God knows all hearts, and he sees you. He keeps watch over your soul, and he knows you knew! *Proverbs 24:12*

CONFRONTED BY GOD FOR HIS SIN, Adam's first response was to blame Eve. Pilate also tried to deflect responsibility for sentencing Jesus to death. That is often the pattern in our world. Rather than take responsibility for their own actions, people prefer to blame someone or something else. God says we are responsible for our own conduct. Be courageous—take responsibility for yourself, and you will be more motivated to do what is right.

GOD'S CHALLENGE

We are each responsible for our own conduct.
Galatians 6:5

COURAGE

How can I stand courageously for God?

GOD'S RESPONSE

I heard the LORD asking, "Whom should I send as a messenger to my people? Who will go for us?" And I said, "Lord, I'll go! Send me."   *Isaiah 6:8*

When Daniel learned that the law [against praying to anyone but the king] had been signed, he went home and knelt down as usual in his upstairs room, with its windows open toward Jerusalem. He prayed three times a day, just as he had always done.   *Daniel 6:10*

G OD HAS GIVEN YOU THE FREEDOM to make your own choices and it is your responsibility to make the right ones. Choose to stand up for God and his way of life. Be fiercely committed to obeying his Word no matter what, and live out the purpose he has for your life even in the face of great danger. Follow God fearlessly and serve him faithfully, like the prophets of old. Be the one to take a stand so that others will be inspired to follow.

GOD'S PROMISE

To those who use well what they are given, even more will be given.   *Matthew 25:29*

COURAGE

Where do I get the courage to deal with life's obstacles?

GOD'S RESPONSE

The LORD your God . . . is with you!   *Deuteronomy 20:1*

The LORD is my light and my salvation—so why should I be afraid?   *Psalm 27:1*

Don't be afraid, for I am with you. Do not be dismayed, for I am your God. I will strengthen you. I will help you. I will uphold you with my victorious right hand.   *Isaiah 41:10*

Be strong and very courageous. Obey all the laws Moses gave you. Do not turn away from them, and you will be successful in everything you do.   *Joshua 1:7*

THE MORE CONVINCED YOU ARE that you can over-come an obstacle, the more boldly you will attack it. If you are convinced that God will help you overcome your obstacles, then you will be even more courageous in moving ahead. This conviction that God will help comes mostly from reading and studying God's Word, where you discover his desire and power to accomplish great things through you.

GOD'S PROMISE

Humanly speaking, it is impossible. But with God everything is possible.   *Matthew 19:26*

COURAGE

Are there models of courage to inspire me?

GOD'S RESPONSE

Again he left them and prayed, "My Father! If this cup cannot be taken away until I drink it, your will be done." *Matthew 26:42*

"Don't worry about a thing," David told Saul. "I'll go fight this Philistine!"   *1 Samuel 17:32*

Paul called the crew together and said, . . . "None of you will lose your lives, even though the ship will go down. . . . Take courage! For I believe God."   *Acts 27:21-22, 25*

O THER BELIEVERS WHO HAVE OVERCOME struggles can inspire us to be bold in the face of our own trials. However, Jesus' response to the prospect of his death on the cross is our greatest model of courage. He understood fear, but he accepted the troubles ahead because he knew he was accomplishing God's plan for him. Courage does not always mean fearlessness. Courage is stepping out in faith in spite of your fear and trusting God to fulfill his plan for you as you faithfully trust and follow him.

GOD'S PROMISE

You will have courage because you will have hope. *Job 11:18*

CONTENTMENT

How can I be content when the world is telling me I can "have it all"?

GOD'S RESPONSE

True godliness with contentment is itself great wealth. After all, we brought nothing with us when we came into the world, and we can't take anything with us when we leave it. *1 Timothy 6:6-7 (NLT2)*

I have learned how to get along happily whether I have much or little. I know how to live on almost nothing or with everything. *Philippians 4:11-12*

D ESPITE OVERWHELMING EVIDENCE to the contrary, most people still believe that money brings happiness. How can you avoid the love of money? Here are some guidelines: (1) Realize that one day your riches will all be gone; (2) Learn to be content with what you have; (3) Monitor what you are willing to do to get more money; (4) Love people more than money; (5) Love God's work more than money; and (6) Freely share what you have with others.

GOD'S PROMISE

Let them praise the LORD for his great love and for all his wonderful deeds to them. For he satisfies the thirsty and fills the hungry with good things. *Psalm 107:8-9*

WEALTH

What is the relationship between wealth and contentment?

GOD'S RESPONSE

Tell those who are rich in this world not to be proud and not to trust in their money, which will soon be gone. But their trust should be in the living God, who richly gives us all we need for our enjoyment.   *1 Timothy 6:17*

Those who love money will never have enough. How absurd to think that wealth brings true happiness! *Ecclesiastes 5:10*

Trust in your money and down you go!   *Proverbs 11:28*

M ONEY AND POSSESSIONS can easily deceive you into thinking, If only I had a little more, I would be content. Nothing could be further from the truth. Always wanting a bit more is a sign of discontent. Contentment is not based on how much material wealth you have, but on how much spiritual wealth you have. If you look to money to make you feel content, you will always be disappointed.

GOD'S CHALLENGE

No one can serve two masters. . . . You cannot serve both God and money.   *Matthew 6:24*

MONEY

What is a proper perspective toward money?

GOD'S RESPONSE

If we have enough food and clothing, let us be content. But people who long to be rich fall into temptation and are trapped by many foolish and harmful desires that plunge them into ruin and destruction. For the love of money is at the root of all kinds of evil. And some people, craving money, have wandered from the faith and pierced themselves with many sorrows.   *1 Timothy 6:8-10*

MONEY CAN BE DANGEROUS because it represents wealth, power, and status. It can wield extraordinary influence. The Bible says that money itself is not sinful, but that the love of money leads to sin. Money must never take the place of God. Instead of viewing money as yours to use as you wish, view it as God's, to use as he wishes. God understands the importance of providing for the needs of your family and for the future, as well as of enjoying life with family and friends. He also expects you to generously help others.

GOD'S CHALLENGE

Give me neither poverty nor riches! Give me just enough to satisfy my needs.   *Proverbs 30:8*

GIVING

How much money should I give away?

GOD'S RESPONSE

Honor the LORD with your wealth and with the best part of everything your land produces.   *Proverbs 3:9*

You must each make up your own mind as to how much you should give. Don't give reluctantly or in response to pressure. For God loves the person who gives cheerfully.
2 Corinthians 9:7

OLD TESTAMENT LAW MADE IT CLEAR that God wanted his people to tithe, to give him the first tenth of their income to demonstrate their obedience and their trust in him to provide for their needs. When Jesus came, he made it clear that he loves a cheerful giver. This means that he loves a generous heart. Whatever the amount, you should honor the Lord with your wealth so that his work on earth can boldly continue. God promises to bless us just as lavishly as we give to him.

GOD'S CHALLENGE

Whatever measure you use in giving—large or small—it will be used to measure what is given back to you.
Luke 6:38

MATERIALISM

How can I avoid a materialistic lifestyle?

GOD'S RESPONSE

Sell what you have and give to those in need. This will store up treasure for you in heaven! And the purses of heaven have no holes in them. Your treasure will be safe—no thief can steal it and no moth can destroy it.   *Luke 12:33*

B ECAUSE PEOPLE HAVE an enormous passion for wanting more things, materialism has great power to turn them away from the Lord. The problem is not with the things themselves, but with a focus on acquiring and managing wealth that begins to consume all your time and push God out of your life. Take another look at what is really valuable. Investing money for the future is important, but investing in God's work and in the lives of others pays dividends for eternity. Your monetary investments become worthless to you when you die—none of them can go with you. Consider the spiritual investments you have made. What treasures have you been storing up for eternity?

GOD'S PROMISE

This world is fading away, along with everything it craves. But if you do the will of God, you will live forever.   *1 John 2:17*

NEEDS

I've made some bad financial decisions.
Will God still help me deal with my debt?

GOD'S RESPONSE

Don't worry about having enough food or drink or clothing. Why be like the pagans who are so deeply concerned about these things? Your heavenly Father already knows all your needs, and he will give you all you need from day to day if you live for him and make the Kingdom of God your primary concern.   *Matthew 6:31-33*

YOU WILL HONOR GOD if you make a budget so that you live within your means and pay off your debt. God wants to help free you from the burden of heavy debt because it makes you worry and distracts you from him. Ask God for wisdom. He knows your needs and will help you meet them if you are willing to make the needed sacrifices.

GOD'S PROMISE

"Bring all the tithes into the storehouse. . . . If you do," says the LORD Almighty, "I will open the windows of heaven for you. I will pour out a blessing so great you won't have enough room to take it in! Try it! Let me prove it to you!"   *Malachi 3:10*

PANIC

The worries in my life are causing me to panic.
How can I overcome these fears?

GOD'S RESPONSE

As Pharaoh and his army approached . . . the people began to panic, and they cried out to the Lord for help. Then they turned against Moses and complained, "Why did you bring us out here to die in the wilderness?"   *Exodus 14:10-11*

Call on me when you are in trouble, and I will rescue you, and you will give me glory.   *Psalm 50:15 (NLT2)*

PANIC IS THE FEELING that an overwhelming crisis is looming and you have no control. These verses make the situation clear. God's job is to rescue you. Your job is to trust God and then to give God glory. What a beautiful picture! Troubles are an occasion to experience God's peace, not panic. Often, though, we get things exactly backwards. We make matters worse by expecting God to trust us to rescue ourselves so that we get the glory. A key to success in all of life—and especially when facing challenges—is to give things over to God that are out of your control.

GOD'S PROMISE

I prayed to the Lord, and he answered me, freeing me from all my fears.   *Psalm 34:4*

TROUBLE

How can I deal with stress so that it has a positive effect in my life?

GOD'S RESPONSE

Dear brothers and sisters, whenever trouble comes your way, let it be an opportunity for joy. For when your faith is tested, your endurance has a chance to grow. So let it grow, for when your endurance is fully developed, you will be strong in character and ready for anything. *James 1:2-4*

Give your burdens to the LORD, and he will take care of you. He will not permit the godly to slip and fall. *Psalm 55:22*

STRESS PUTS GREAT PRESSURE on your health and relationships. It is a warning sign that you are being stretched to your limit, and that beyond that limit you will snap. But stress can be positive if you learn and grow from it. Just as a muscle can only grow under pressure, so your wisdom and character can only grow under the pressures of life. As you look for what God is teaching you in your stressful times, you will become better equipped to deal with other stressful situations.

GOD'S PROMISE

I will call to you whenever trouble strikes, and you will answer me. *Psalm 86:7*

PROVISION

Does God really care about my daily needs?

GOD'S RESPONSE

This same God who takes care of me will supply all your needs from his glorious riches, which have been given to us in Christ Jesus.   *Philippians 4:19*

God will generously provide all you need. Then you will always have everything you need and plenty left over to share with others. As the Scriptures say, "Godly people give generously to the poor."   *2 Corinthians 9:8-9*

WE MUST LEARN TO DISTINGUISH between wants and needs. When we understand what we truly need and we see how God provides, we will realize how much he truly cares for us. God doesn't promise to give you lots of possessions, but rather to help you possess the character traits that reflect his nature so that you can accomplish his plan for you. He doesn't promise to preserve your physical life. He will preserve your soul in a new body for all eternity if you pledge your allegiance to him.

GOD'S PROMISE

I will be your God throughout your lifetime—until your hair is white with age. I made you, and I will care for you.   *Isaiah 46:4*

GIVING

Why does God promise to meet my needs?

GOD'S RESPONSE

One day a man from Baal-shalishah brought [Elisha] a sack of fresh grain and twenty loaves of barley bread made from the first grain of his harvest. Elisha said, "Give it to the group of prophets so they can eat."

"What?" his servant exclaimed. "Feed one hundred people with only this?"

But Elisha repeated, "Give it to the group of prophets so they can eat, for the LORD says there will be plenty for all. There will even be some left over!" And sure enough, there was plenty for all and some left over, just as the LORD had promised.   *2 Kings 4:42-44*

GOD GIVES TO YOU so that you will be satisfied and able to give to others. Whether you have been richly blessed or have just enough to get by, the Lord promises that there will always be enough to share. Give generously and watch God work with it!

GOD'S CHALLENGE

Don't forget to do good and to share what you have with those in need, for such sacrifices are very pleasing to God.   *Hebrews 13:16*

SUCCESS

How can I be successful?

GOD'S RESPONSE

Be careful to obey all the instructions Moses gave you. Do not deviate from them, turning either to the right or to the left. Then you will be successful in everything you do. *Joshua 1:7 (NLT2)*

Commit your work to the LORD, and then your plans will succeed.   *Proverbs 16:3*

THROUGHOUT THE BIBLE, complete obedience to God's Word is the key to success. Conversely, selective obedience undermines success, for it lulls us into thinking that we have fully obeyed. A "little sin" is still a sin, and a little disobedience is still disobedience (read James 2:10). God urges us to keep all of his laws. We can fall into the trap of thinking that we are good Christians because we follow God's commands generally, while in fact we are ignoring or revising certain commands that seem inconvenient. Selective obedience is obeying on our terms; full obedience is obeying on God's terms. Are you sold out to God?

GOD'S PROMISE

Happy are those who fear the LORD. Yes, happy are those who delight in doing what he commands.   *Psalm 112:1*

PROVISION

Besides basic physical needs, what other types of needs does God promise to supply?

GOD'S RESPONSE

He is the kind of high priest we need because he is holy and blameless, unstained by sin.   *Hebrews 7:26*

When I pray, you answer me; you encourage me by giving me the strength I need.   *Psalm 138:3*

One day the apostles said to the Lord, "We need more faith; tell us how to get it."   *Luke 17:5*

God is faithful. He will keep the temptation from becoming so strong that you can't stand up against it. When you are tempted, he will show you a way out so that you will not give in to it.   *1 Corinthians 10:13*

THERE ARE SOME NEEDS that God promises always to meet. God will always meet your need for salvation, mercy, wisdom, comfort, strength, a way out of temptation, and faith. He does that through the Holy Spirit.

GOD'S PROMISE

Since God did not spare even his own Son but gave him up for us all, won't God, who gave us Christ, also give us everything else?   *Romans 8:32*

RELIABILITY

Can I really trust God to keep his promises?

GOD'S RESPONSE

God also bound himself with an oath, so that those who received the promise could be perfectly sure that he would never change his mind. So God has given us both his promise and his oath. These two things are unchangeable because it is impossible for God to lie. Therefore, we who have fled to him for refuge can take new courage, for we can hold on to his promise with confidence.   *Hebrews 6:17-18*

FAITH REQUIRES TRUST, and trust is believing something to be true and then acting on that belief. If you believe in God, you will believe his promises. Then you will base your entire life on what God says and trust his promises to be true. To do this you must see your problems through God's eyes and then move forward in faith. You must not ignore God's promises or discourage others from believing in them (read Numbers 13:31-33). Trusting God's promises and acting upon them will move your life in the right direction. It will also spur others to move forward in their faith as they see the blessings that come from faithful living.

GOD'S PROMISE

God can be trusted to keep his promise.   *Hebrews 10:23*

GOD'S PROMISES

How can God's promises change the way I live?

GOD'S RESPONSE

When God promised Abraham that he would become the father of many nations, Abraham believed him. . . . And Abraham's faith did not weaken, even though he knew that he was too old to be a father at the age of one hundred and that Sarah, his wife, had never been able to have children. Abraham never wavered in believing God's promise. In fact, his faith grew stronger, and in this he brought glory to God. He was absolutely convinced that God was able to do anything he promised. *Romans 4:18-21*

WHEN YOU ARE ABSOLUTELY CONVINCED that God is able to do anything he promises, then the troubles of this world are put in perspective. When you are absolutely convinced that God will keep his promises, you will follow him without hesitation. And when you follow him, you will have peace no matter what happens.

GOD'S PROMISE

God has given us both his promise and his oath. These two things are unchangeable because it is impossible for God to lie. Therefore, we who have fled to him for refuge can take new courage, for we can hold on to his promise with confidence. *Hebrews 6:18*

POWER

What is God's power like?

GOD'S RESPONSE

Jesus got into the boat and started across the lake with his disciples. Suddenly, a fierce storm struck the lake. . . . "Lord, save us! We're going to drown!" Jesus responded, "Why are you afraid?" . . . He got up and rebuked the wind and waves, and suddenly there was a great calm. The disciples were amazed. "Who is this man?" they asked. "Even the wind and waves obey him!" *Matthew 8:23-27 (NLT2)*

IMAGINE THE EARTH'S STRONGEST EARTHQUAKE, tallest tsunami, wildest volcano, and most devastating hurricane—all in one place. This cannot even begin to compare to God's power because he is the creator of all these phenomena, and the created is never more powerful than the creator. This same God who can instantly calm the storm over the Sea of Galilee has the power to calm the storms in your heart, dry up your flood of fear, quench the fires of lust, and control the whirlwind of your life. Are you a man who believes in the power of God, or do you feel more comfortable taking matters into your own hands?

GOD'S PROMISE

You are my King and my God. . . . It is you who gives us victory. *Psalm 44:4, 7*

POWER

How can I experience God's power working through me?

GOD'S RESPONSE

This is the secret: Christ lives in you, and this is your assurance that you will share in his glory. . . . I work very hard at this, as I depend on Christ's mighty power that works within me.   *Colossians 1:27, 29*

Each time he said, "My gracious favor is all you need. My power works best in your weakness." So now I am glad to boast about my weaknesses, so that the power of Christ may work through me.   *2 Corinthians 12:9*

THE MORE YOU RECOGNIZE your weaknesses and limitations, the more you need God's power at work in you. Strength can make you proud and self-sufficient. You don't feel that you need to rely much on God or others when you are very good at something or have great authority. That is why God often works through our weaknesses—if we let him—because then there is no doubt that it is by his power and not our own that the task is getting done.

GOD'S PROMISE

God is working in you, giving you the desire to obey him and the power to do what pleases him.   *Philippians 2:13*

DISTRESS

What should I do when I am distressed?

GOD'S RESPONSE

The Israelites did what was evil in the LORD's sight. . . . They abandoned the LORD. . . . He sold them to their enemies all around, and they were no longer able to resist them. Every time Israel went out to battle, the LORD fought against them, bringing them defeat, just as he promised. And the people were very distressed.   *Judges 2:11-12, 14-15*

CERTAIN ACTIONS have predictable reactions. God's Word makes it clear that sin always hurts us because it separates us from God (our source of mercy and blessing). Giving in to temptation puts us in the middle of the road where evil hurtles toward us at high speed. Being run over by the consequences of sin causes great distress in our lives. Not all distress is caused by our sinful actions, but the next time you are distressed, as the people of Israel were, your first response should be to check to see if there are areas of your life in which you are giving in to sin. Then get off the road of temptation, return to the Lord, and cry for his mercy. God has a soft spot for humble and repentant people.

GOD'S PROMISE

I cry out to God Most High, to God who will fulfill his purpose for me.   *Psalm 57:2*

FEAR OF GOD

What does it mean to fear the Lord?

GOD'S RESPONSE

Let us work toward complete purity because we fear God.
2 Corinthians 7:1

MANY WORDS IN THE ENGLISH LANGUAGE have several strikingly different definitions. For example, anger can mean unbridled temper or it can mean righteous indignation. Love can mean lust or unconditional commitment. Normally we think of fear as an unpleasant emotion tied to anxious concern or outright terror of being harmed. But there is another definition of fear that can lead to something good and wonderful. The fear of God is complete awe and respect for him, a realization that everything he says about love and justice is true. Because God is great and mighty, and because he holds the power of life and death in his hands, a healthy and reverent fear of him helps us to respond to him as we should. This draws us closer to him and to the blessings he gives.

GOD'S PROMISE

Don't be afraid, for I am with you. Do not be dismayed, for I am your God. I will strengthen you. I will help you. I will uphold you with my victorious right hand.
Isaiah 41:10

FAITH

How can I become stronger in my faith?

GOD'S RESPONSE

Teach the older men to exercise self-control, to be worthy of respect, and to live wisely. They must have strong faith and be filled with love and patience.   *Titus 2:2*

Be careful to obey every command I am giving you today, so you may have strength to go in and occupy the land you are about to enter.   *Deuteronomy 11:8*

JUST AS YOUR MUSCLES GET STRONGER with exercise, so your faith gets stronger the more you exercise it. To strengthen your faith, spend time in training with God each day, being careful to obey his regimen for healthy and godly living. Then your faith will be strengthened and your spiritual muscles will be ready to take on whatever life throws at you.

GOD'S CHALLENGE

Physical exercise has some value, but spiritual exercise is much more important, for it promises a reward in both this life and the next.   *1 Timothy 4:8*

STRENGTH

What are the signs of spiritual strength?

GOD'S RESPONSE

If we are thrown into the blazing furnace, the God whom we serve is able to save us. He will rescue us from your power. . . . But even if he doesn't, Your Majesty can be sure that we will never serve your gods.   *Daniel 3:17-18*

Be strong and courageous! Don't be afraid of the king of Assyria or his mighty army, for there is a power far greater on our side! He may have a great army, but they are just men. We have the LORD our God to help us and to fight our battles for us!   *2 Chronicles 32:7-8*

SCRIPTURE PROVIDES RADICAL EXAMPLES of spiritual strength through bravery in battle and daring opposition to evil. Other signs of spiritual strength include extreme dependence on God, humility, gentleness, peace, self-control, and a passion for serving others. Ultimately, spiritual strength is a determined, consistent commitment to following God, both publicly and privately, no matter what.

GOD'S PROMISE

It is not that we think we can do anything of lasting value by ourselves. Our only power and success come from God.   *2 Corinthians 3:5*

PROBLEMS

How does God's strength help me with my problems?

GOD'S RESPONSE

There is wonderful joy ahead, even though it is necessary for you to endure many trials for a while. These trials are only to test your faith, to show that it is strong and pure. It is being tested as fire tests and purifies gold—and your faith is far more precious to God than mere gold. So if your faith remains strong after being tried by fiery trials, it will bring you much praise and glory and honor on the day when Jesus Christ is revealed to the whole world.   *1 Peter 1:6-7*

THE NEXT TIME YOU FACE TROUBLE or hardship, see it as an opportunity to rely on God for strength and endurance. If you can trust him with your pain, confusion, and loneliness, you will win a spiritual victory because you will have defended yourself against the temptation of the enemy to let anger, bitterness, or discouragement defeat you. God never promised to make your life easy; he did promise to be with you and to make your faith strong and pure through the trials and troubles of your life.

GOD'S CHALLENGE

Abraham never wavered in believing God's promise. In fact, his faith grew stronger, and in this he brought glory to God.   *Romans 4:20*

PRAYER

How does prayer help me to tap into God's power?

GOD'S RESPONSE

Keep on asking, and you will be given what you ask for. . . . For everyone who asks, receives. . . . If you sinful people know how to give good gifts to your children, how much more will your heavenly Father give good gifts to those who ask him.   *Matthew 7:7-8, 11*

THERE'S MORE TO PRAYER than just getting an answer. As you persist in prayer, you gain a greater understanding of yourself and your motivations, and whether or not they are aligned with God's direction for your life. God wants to use you in bringing about his will in the world, and this involves your seeking his will and not your own. Communication with God through prayer is necessary if you want his power for living.

GOD'S CHALLENGE

Pray for each other so that you may be healed. The earnest prayer of a righteous person has great power and wonderful results.   *James 5:16*

LISTENING

How can I know that God hears my prayers?

GOD'S RESPONSE

The eyes of the Lord watch over those who do right, and his ears are open to their prayers.   *1 Peter 3:12*

The LORD is far from the wicked, but he hears the prayers of the righteous.   *Proverbs 15:29*

SOMETIMES IT FEELS AS IF OUR PRAYERS are bouncing off the ceiling. Is God paying attention? The bigger question is: Are you paying attention to God's response? God does answer prayer, and he wants to do so because he is loving and good. It's his nature to give good things to his people. Sometimes, after things work out, we fail to give God the credit because we didn't notice that he answered! When you pray, be alert and watch for God's response, even if it isn't what you expected. And then don't forget to thank him for it, no matter what it is, because you can be confident that it is in your best interest.

GOD'S PROMISE

We can be confident that he will listen to us whenever we ask him for anything in line with his will.
1 John 5:14

ANSWERS

Does God always answer prayer?

GOD'S RESPONSE

I love the LORD because he hears and answers my prayers.
Psalm 116:1

Three different times I begged the Lord to take it away.
Each time he said, . . . "My power works best in your
weakness." *2 Corinthians 12:8-9*

Confess your sins to each other and pray for each other so
that you may be healed. The earnest prayer of a righteous
person has great power and wonderful results. *James 5:16*

G OD ALWAYS LISTENS AND RESPONDS to your prayers.
However, his answers may not always be what you
expect. As your loving heavenly Father who knows what
is best, he does not always give you what you ask for. You
can trust his answer of yes, no, or wait. Sometimes, like
Paul, you will find that God answers prayer by giving you
something better than you asked for.

GOD'S PROMISE

The eyes of the Lord watch over those who do right,
and his ears are open to their prayers. *1 Peter 3:12*

COMMUNICATION

*What does God desire in my communication
with him?*

GOD'S RESPONSE

If my people who are called by my name will humble
themselves and pray and seek my face and turn from their
wicked ways, I will hear from heaven.   *2 Chronicles 7:14*

O my people, trust in him at all times. Pour out your
heart to him, for God is our refuge.   *Psalm 62:8*

Keep on praying.   *1 Thessalonians 5:17*

G OD HONORS THE HUMBLE and acknowledges their
prayers (1 Peter 5:6; Daniel 10:12). When you come
to God in humility, your prayers are more aligned with his
plans for you because you recognize that he is sovereign.
His will for your life will lead you toward what is good
and right and away from sin and harm. Before you step
out boldly, fall to your knees humbly.

GOD'S PROMISE

I think how much you have helped me; I sing for joy
in the shadow of your protecting wings. I follow close
behind you; your strong right hand holds me securely.
Psalm 63:7-8

ROUTINE

How can I make prayer a part of my daily routine?

GOD'S RESPONSE

When I heard this, I sat down and wept. In fact, for days I mourned, fasted, and prayed to the God of heaven. *Nehemiah 1:4*

The king asked, "Well, how can I help you?" With a prayer to the God of heaven, I replied.   *Nehemiah 2:4-5*

I prayed for strength to continue the work.   *Nehemiah 6:9*

TAKE A LESSON FROM NEHEMIAH. He communicated at length with God through prayer and fasting. At other times, he shot prayers to God at a moment's notice when he needed God's help in an urgent matter. He prayed for protection and strength. Making prayer a habit begins with consciously making time for prayer, but after a while it will become second nature as you walk and talk with God throughout the day.

GOD'S CHALLENGE

Ezra praised the LORD, the great God, and all the people chanted, "Amen! Amen!" as they lifted their hands toward heaven. Then they bowed down and worshiped the LORD with their faces to the ground.   *Nehemiah 8:6*

COMMUNICATION

How does God communicate with me?

GOD'S RESPONSE

Long ago God spoke many times and in many ways to our ancestors through the prophets. But now in these final days, he has spoken to us through his Son. *Hebrews 1:1-2*

The heavens tell of the glory of God. The skies display his marvelous craftsmanship. Day after day they continue to speak; night after night they make him known. *Psalm 19:1-2*

GOD SPEAKS THROUGH HIS WORD, so read it daily. He speaks through his Son, Jesus, so talk to him daily. He speaks through his Holy Spirit, so pause to listen as he counsels your heart and mind. He speaks through his creation, so take time to see him in it. And he speaks through other people, so be fed through the teaching, preaching, and advice of other believers. Listening to all the ways God speaks to you is the best way to discover his unchanging qualities and his purposes for your life.

GOD'S PROMISE

Fear of the LORD is the foundation of true knowledge. *Proverbs 1:7 (NLT2)*

OBEDIENCE

How does God want me to obey him?

GOD'S RESPONSE

Obey me, and I will be your God, and you will be my people. Only do as I say, and all will be well! *Jeremiah 7:23*

Thank God! Once you were slaves of sin, but now you have obeyed with all your heart the new teaching God has given you. *Romans 6:17*

OBEDIENCE IS DEFINED as "being submissive to an authority." We all obey an authority, be it our own rules, the rules of the world, or the ways of God. Ironically, obedience to God's ways actually frees you to enjoy life as he originally created it, keeping you from becoming entangled or enslaved to the sinful things that distract or hurt you. It protects you from the evil that God knows is there, leads you on right paths where you will find blessing, and directs you into service that will please him.

GOD'S PROMISE

If you keep looking steadily into God's perfect law—the law that sets you free—and if you do what it says and don't forget what you heard, then God will bless you for doing it. *James 1:25*

EMPOWERMENT

I want to obey, but it's difficult.
How will God help me?

GOD'S RESPONSE

If you love me, obey my commandments. And I will ask
the Father, and he will give you another Counselor, who
will never leave you.   *John 14:15-16*

Keep alert and pray. Otherwise temptation will overpower
you.   *Matthew 26:41*

W HEN GOD REQUIRES, he also empowers. When
Jesus faced troubles, he found a quiet place, away
from the crowd, and prayed to God for strength. Follow
Jesus' example and first remove yourself from temptation
and then ask God for help. You also have the aid of the
Holy Spirit, who comes alongside you in your time of
need. Even as the air you breathe empowers your body to
function, so the Holy Spirit empowers your spirit to obey.

GOD'S PROMISE

If you keep looking steadily into God's perfect law—the
law that sets you free—and if you do what it says and
don't forget what you heard, then God will bless you for
doing it.   *James 1:25*

CONFESSION

When should we confess our sins?

GOD'S RESPONSE

When any of the people become aware of their guilt in any of these ways, they must confess their sin.   *Leviticus 5:5*

Confess your sins to each other and pray for each other so that you may be healed. The earnest prayer of a righteous person has great power and wonderful results.   *James 5:16*

G OD OFTEN USES THE FEELING OF GUILT in your conscience to help you know that it is time to apologize or confess to wrongdoing. Sinning shamelessly, without a sense of guilt, is an act of shutting God out. If you have no desire to have your sins forgiven, God will not forgive them. Ask God to reveal actions and thoughts that displease him. Do you feel guilty about something you have said or done to hurt another person? It's time to apologize and seek forgiveness. Confession indicates your desire to have your sins forgiven. What results from your confession? God removes your guilt, restores your joy, and heals your broken soul.

GOD'S PROMISE

People who cover over their sins will not prosper. But if they confess and forsake them, they will receive mercy.
Proverbs 28:13

WORDS

When I speak to God and to others, do my words really matter?

GOD'S RESPONSE

If you claim to be religious but don't control your tongue, you are just fooling yourself, and your religion is worthless. *James 1:26*

A gentle answer turns away wrath, but harsh words stir up anger.   *Proverbs 15:1*

W HAT COMES OUT OF YOUR MOUTH shows what is in your heart. Your words show what kind of person you really are. Criticism, gossip, flattery, lying, and profanity are not only "word" problems, but "heart" problems as well. Being more careful with your words isn't enough. You must first have a change of heart, and then good, kind, and healing words will follow.

GOD'S CHALLENGE

Who may worship in your sanctuary, LORD? Who may enter your presence on your holy hill? Those who lead blameless lives and do what is right, speaking the truth from sincere hearts. Those who refuse to slander others or harm their neighbors or speak evil of their friends. *Psalm 15:1-3*

TEMPTATION

Is being tempted the same as sinning?

GOD'S RESPONSE

Since he himself has gone through suffering and temptation, he is able to help us when we are being tempted.   *Hebrews 2:18*

Watch out for attacks from the Devil, your great enemy. He prowls around like a roaring lion, looking for some victim to devour. Take a firm stand against him, and be strong in your faith.   *1 Peter 5:8-9*

JESUS FACED TEMPTATIONS and never gave in. Since Jesus was sinless, being tempted is different from sinning. You don't have to feel guilty about temptations that come into your life because sometimes you cannot control them. However, you can feel guilty when you give in to temptation. Satan is always trying to make you stumble. Sometimes you must literally run from temptation straight to Jesus so he can give you strength to fight against it.

GOD'S CHALLENGE

No one who wants to do wrong should ever say, "God is tempting me." God is never tempted to do wrong, and he never tempts anyone else either.   *James 1:13*

TEMPTATION

Where does temptation come from?

GOD'S RESPONSE

Temptation comes from the lure of our own evil desires.
James 1:14

ALL TEMPTATION ULTIMATELY comes from Satan. He almost always makes sin look lovely, seductive, attractive, and even fun because he knows our vulnerabilities and he loves to strike at our weakest places. Temptation is planted and nurtured in the soil of your sinful nature, and since no human can completely resist all temptation, you must be ruthless to weed out any sinful habit. Otherwise, it will grow out of control before you know it and begin to choke out your character, integrity, and reputation. Beg God for the power not to give temptation a second look.

GOD'S PROMISE

Since he himself has gone through suffering and temptation, he is able to help us when we are being tempted.   *Hebrews 2:18*

ESCAPE

Can Satan force me to sin?

GOD'S RESPONSE

Remember that the temptations that come into your life are no different from what others experience. And God is faithful. He will keep the temptation from becoming so strong that you can't stand up against it. When you are tempted, he will show you a way out so that you will not give in to it.   *1 Corinthians 10:13*

Resist the Devil, and he will flee from you.   *James 4:7*

DON'T UNDERESTIMATE the power of Satan, but don't overestimate it either. He can tempt you, but he cannot force you to sin. He can dangle the bait in front of you, but he cannot make you take it. The Bible promises that no temptation will ever be too strong for you to resist. Even in times of heavy temptation, God provides a way out. In these times of temptation, the Holy Spirit gives you the power and the wisdom to find the way of escape.

GOD'S PROMISE

All glory to God, who is able to keep you from falling away and will bring you with great joy into his glorious presence without a single fault.   *Jude 1:24* (NLT2)

RESISTANCE

How can I resist temptation?

GOD'S RESPONSE

He ran from the house.   *Genesis 39:12*

Daniel made up his mind not to defile himself by eating the food.   *Daniel 1:8*

Follow my advice, my son; always treasure my commands. Obey them and live! Guard my teachings as your most precious possession. Tie them on your fingers as a reminder. Write them deep within your heart. Love wisdom like a sister; make insight a beloved member of your family. Let them hold you back from an affair with an immoral woman, from listening to the flattery of an adulterous woman.   *Proverbs 7:1-5*

THE BEST TIME TO PREPARE for temptation is before it presses into you. Train yourself in the quieter times so that you will have the spiritual wisdom, strength, and commitment to honor God in the face of intense desires and temptation. Sometimes you may have to resist temptation by running away.

GOD'S CHALLENGE

Above all else, guard your heart, for it affects everything you do.   *Proverbs 4:23*

RECOVERY

How do I recover when I have given in to temptation?

GOD'S RESPONSE

Do not banish me from your presence, and don't take your Holy Spirit from me. Restore to me again the joy of your salvation, and make me willing to obey you. Then I will teach your ways to sinners, and they will return to you. . . . You would not be pleased with sacrifices, or I would bring them. . . . The sacrifice you want is a broken spirit. A broken and repentant heart, O God, you will not despise.   *Psalm 51:11-13, 16-17*

G OD'S GRACE IS GREATER than your failure. Temptation only wins when it keeps you from turning back to God. No matter how often you fail, God welcomes you back through the love of Jesus Christ. Recovery begins when you return to God. He will not despise your broken and repentant heart. He promises to welcome you back, to forgive you, and to help you start over.

GOD'S PROMISE

It was necessary for Jesus to be in every respect like us. . . . He then could offer a sacrifice that would take away the sins of the people.   *Hebrews 2:17*

THOUGHTS

How can I discipline my mind and thoughts?

GOD'S RESPONSE

I will study your commandments and reflect on your ways.
Psalm 119:15

Fix your thoughts on what is true and honorable and right.
Think about things that are pure and lovely and admirable.
Think about things that are excellent and worthy of praise.
Philippians 4:8

TRY TO THINK ABOUT WHAT IS true, honorable, right, pure, lovely, and admirable. You can do that by committing God's Word to memory or inviting God into your thought life to make you more accountable. Be open for him to radically change the way you think. When you dwell on the good in your life, and all you have to be thankful for, you won't have room for anything else.

GOD'S CHALLENGE

Search me, O God, and know my heart; test me and know my thoughts. Point out anything in me that offends you, and lead me along the path of everlasting life.   *Psalm 139:23-24*

THOUGHTS

How do my thoughts affect my actions?

GOD'S RESPONSE

You have heard that the law of Moses says, "Do not commit adultery." But I say, anyone who even looks at a woman with lust in his eye has already committed adultery with her in his heart. *Matthew 5:27-28*

THE HEART IS LIKE A COMPUTER CHIP that runs your life. It is the center of your passions, desires, and beliefs. From your heart come your thoughts and actions. Since all people are born with a sinful nature (Romans 3:23), the heart is naturally corrupt. Therefore, to replace your sinful nature with God's new nature, you must be deliberate about forcing out anything that takes the place of God and consistently tempts you. God cannot occupy your heart and redeem it if someone or something else already lives there that you are more passionate about. Is God affecting your thoughts and actions, or are you allowing something else to control you?

GOD'S CHALLENGE

The godly think before speaking; the wicked spout evil words. *Proverbs 15:28*

MOTIVES

Does God care about my motives as long as I do the right thing?

GOD'S RESPONSE

The Lord accepted Abel and his offering, but he did not accept Cain and his offering.   *Genesis 4:4-5*

Don't do your good deeds publicly, to be admired, because then you will lose the reward from your Father in heaven.   *Matthew 6:1*

People may think they are doing what is right, but the Lord examines the heart.   *Proverbs 21:2*

I T IS QUITE LIKELY THAT CAIN'S SACRIFICE was regarded as inappropriate because his motives were impure. David's motive in taking the census—probably to see how powerful he had become—displeased God. Your motives matter to God because they expose whether you're working for God or for yourself. When you pursue your spiritual life with self-serving motives, you rob yourself of the joy God intends and the relationship he desires.

GOD'S CHALLENGE

Put me on trial, Lord, and cross-examine me. Test my motives and affections.   *Psalm 26:2*

MOTIVES

How can I have pure motives?

GOD'S RESPONSE

The Lord sees every heart and understands and knows every plan and thought.   *1 Chronicles 28:9*

May the words of my mouth and the thoughts of my heart be pleasing to you, O Lord, my rock and my redeemer. *Psalm 19:14*

My conscience is clear, but that isn't what matters. It is the Lord himself who will examine me and decide. *1 Corinthians 4:4*

WHEN OUR MOTIVES ARE SELFISH OR IMPURE, it is only a matter of time before our actions are also selfish and impure. God is far more concerned about the condition of our hearts than he is with our external behavior—our behavior always flows from our hearts, not the other way around. Remember that God alone knows your heart. You may be able to fool others and yourself, but you can't fool God. Welcome his examination. Then you can say, like Paul, that your conscience is clear.

GOD'S CHALLENGE

Fire tests the purity of silver and gold, but the Lord tests the heart.   *Proverbs 17:3*

PRIDE

Why is pride one of the "seven deadly sins" when other things seem so much worse?

GOD'S RESPONSE

When he had become powerful, he also became proud, which led to his downfall.   *2 Chronicles 26:16*

The proud Pharisee stood by himself and prayed this prayer: "I thank you, God, that I am not a sinner like everyone else, especially like that tax collector over there!"   *Luke 18:11*

P RIDE IS THE MAIN REASON for our falling away from God. We become vulnerable to Satan when we believe that we are strong enough to resist his attacks. He loves to prove us wrong. Pride can also creep in when we become prosperous and take the credit for our fine life. We forget the Lord when we have plenty and don't rely on him for food each day. The bottom line on pride boils down to forgetting God. You forget to thank him, to give him credit, and to rely on him. And when you get to that point, your pride will lead to a great fall.

GOD'S CHALLENGE

Pride goes before destruction, and haughtiness before a fall.   *Proverbs 16:18*

PRIDE

Is pride ever appropriate?

GOD'S RESPONSE

It is right for me to be enthusiastic about all Christ Jesus has done through me.   *Romans 15:17*

God alone made it possible for you to be in Christ Jesus. . . . As the Scriptures say, "The person who wishes to boast should boast only of what the Lord has done." *1 Corinthians 1:30-31*

God forbid that I should boast about anything except the cross of our Lord Jesus Christ.   *Galatians 6:14*

P RIDE IS APPROPRIATE WHEN YOU FEEL a grateful satisfaction for what God is doing through you. It's okay to feel pride in a job well done when you have honored God in your task. It's okay to be proud of your children; they are a gift from God. Paul was not proud of what he had accomplished but of what God had done through him. Like Paul, take pride in what the Lord has done. Then your focus is on him and not on yourself.

GOD'S CHALLENGE

Those who exalt themselves will be humbled, and those who humble themselves will be exalted.   *Matthew 23:12*

What can I learn from my anger?

GOD'S RESPONSE

Balaam's donkey suddenly saw the angel of the LORD standing in the road with a drawn sword. . . . It tried to squeeze by and crushed Balaam's foot against the wall. So Balaam beat the donkey. . . . Then the LORD opened Balaam's eyes, and he saw the angel of the LORD. *Numbers 22:23, 25, 31*

"Don't sin by letting anger gain control over you." Don't let the sun go down while you are still angry.   *Ephesians 4:26*

B ALAAM'S ANGER IMMEDIATELY FLARED UP against the donkey. Balaam assumed that he was right and that the problem was the donkey's fault. Fortunately for Balaam, he finally realized that the donkey had saved his life. The next time your pride is hurt and you feel anger rising up within you, don't assume that you are right and everyone else is at fault. Instead of justifying your actions, see whether you can justify your motives. This will tell you if your anger is warranted.

GOD'S PROMISE

The LORD is kind and merciful, slow to get angry, full of unfailing love.   *Psalm 145:8*

LAZINESS

Is laziness a sin?

GOD'S RESPONSE

I walked by the field of a lazy person. . . . I saw that it was overgrown. . . . Its walls were broken down. . . . I learned this lesson: A little extra sleep, a little more slumber, a little folding of the hands to rest—and poverty will pounce on you like a bandit.   *Proverbs 24:30-34*

L AZINESS IS CONSIDERED ONE of the "seven deadly sins," and it is the one most often overlooked. We often think of sin as doing something we should not do, but sin is also the failure to do what we should. Laziness could mean not dealing with your responsibilities, or not confronting someone because you are afraid of the consequences. A lazy person is self-centered and does not want to take time to help out. The spiritually lazy person may fail to notice the approach of temptation. Laziness can be transformed by purpose. Purpose requires courage; you must confront yourself or the enemy and have the discipline to say no to what distracts you from your purpose.

GOD'S CHALLENGE

Work hard and become a leader; be lazy and become a slave.   *Proverbs 12:24*

　　　　　　　　　　　THEFT

In what ways do we steal from others?

GOD'S RESPONSE

I wanted them so much that I took them.　*Joshua 7:21*

When you make an agreement with a neighbor to buy or sell property, you must never take advantage of each other. . . . Show your fear of God by not taking advantage of each other. I, the LORD, am your God.　*Leviticus 25:14, 17*

THE CARTOON VERSION OF A THIEF is usually a sinister figure in a black mask that robs banks, snatches purses, and breaks into homes after dark. Although theft and violent crime are a real part of our world, most of us will be tempted by more subtle and "civilized" forms of stealing, such as padding an expense account, adding false deductions to our income-tax statement, or taking advantage of someone's gullibility or goodness. Whether we rob a widow at knifepoint or skim so smoothly that our victims never know it, stealing is detestable in the eyes of our holy God. Make a commitment to be completely honest in all you do and say.

GOD'S CHALLENGE

You must use accurate scales when you weigh out merchandise. . . . Use honest weights and measures, so that you will enjoy a long life.　*Deuteronomy 25:13-15*

HONESTY

What are the by-products of honesty?

GOD'S RESPONSE

The LORD demands fairness in every business deal; he sets the standard.   *Proverbs 16:11*

If you cheat even a little, you won't be honest with greater responsibilities.   *Luke 16:10*

Good people are guided by their honesty; treacherous people are destroyed by their dishonesty.   *Proverbs 11:3*

HONESTY CREATES TRUST, and trust is the basis of all relationships. God wants you to be completely honest in your life—with him, with yourself, and with others. Your success does not honor God if you cheat or damage others to get ahead. When you are honest in all details, you experience the distinct advantages of a clear conscience, earning the trust and respect of others as well as God's blessing. Make the decision to be honest in all areas of your life.

GOD'S CHALLENGE

Truth stands the test of time; lies are soon exposed.
Proverbs 12:19

REPUTATION

Can a bad reputation be changed?

GOD'S RESPONSE

They will see your honorable behavior, and they will believe and give honor to God.   *1 Peter 2:12*

Some of the brothers recently returned and made me very happy by telling me about your faithfulness and that you are living in the truth.   *3 John 1:3*

TIME INVESTED IN OBEDIENCE TO God results in a reputation that brings honor and respect. Reputation is the yardstick that others use to measure your character—the real you. You can build a good reputation by consistent, godly behavior, and you can start today. Be encouraged by God's promise to redeem any bad situation, and ask God to continue his work in your life so that you can be a living example of the change that Jesus brings to all who trust him.

GOD'S PROMISE

Christians become new persons. They are not the same anymore, for the old life is gone. A new life has begun!
2 Corinthians 5:17

PAST

How can I benefit from the past?

GOD'S RESPONSE

Don't long for "the good old days," for you don't know whether they were any better than today.   *Ecclesiastes 7:10*

No, dear brothers and sisters, I am still not all I should be, but I am focusing all my energies on this one thing: Forgetting the past and looking forward to what lies ahead.   *Philippians 3:13*

Remember the days of long ago; think about the generations past. Ask your father and he will inform you. Inquire of your elders, and they will tell you.   *Deuteronomy 32:7*

W HILE REMEMBERING THE PAST CAN BE HEALTHY, living in the past is not. The past cannot be changed. You can learn from the past so that you don't repeat your mistakes. Your past is most beneficial when you use it to improve your future. Apply the lessons you learn, move forward, and help others to keep from making the same mistakes you did.

GOD'S CHALLENGE

Will not even one of you apply these lessons from the past?   *Isaiah 42:23*

MEMORIES

What is the most effective way to deal with my hurtful past?

GOD'S RESPONSE

Joseph told them, "Don't be afraid of me. Am I God, to judge and punish you? As far as I am concerned, God turned into good what you meant for evil." *Genesis 50:19-20*

Jesus said, "Father, forgive these people, because they don't know what they are doing." *Luke 23:34*

WHEN YOU DWELL ON THE PAST, it is hard to forget it and move on. However, it is important to face it. Deal with the pain of the past in whatever constructive ways you need to—confession, repentance, counseling, forgiveness—and don't feel that you need to do it alone. When you find healthy ways to deal with past hurts, you can receive the blessings God wants to give you today and move joyfully into your future.

GOD'S PROMISE

Among the nations, Judah and Israel had become symbols of what it means to be cursed. But no longer! Now I will rescue you and make you both a symbol and a source of blessing! *Zechariah 8:13*

FORGIVENESS

How should I forgive those who hurt me?

GOD'S RESPONSE

Esau ran to meet him and embraced him affectionately and kissed him. Both of them were in tears.   *Genesis 33:4*

Be kind to each other, tenderhearted, forgiving one another, just as God through Christ has forgiven you.
Ephesians 4:32

Forgive us our sins, just as we have forgiven those who have sinned against us.   *Matthew 6:12*

Stop judging others, and you will not be judged. Stop criticizing others, or it will all come back on you. If you forgive others, you will be forgiven.   *Luke 6:37*

W E FORGIVE OTHERS AS GOD FORGIVES US, which is completely. God's forgiveness is not based on the goodness of the offender or the degree of the offense, but solely on his own loving character. Forgiveness does not erase the offense, but pardons the offender. Forgiveness is a choice, a commitment to reflect God's love for us to others.

GOD'S CHALLENGE

Jesus said, "Father, forgive these people, because they don't know what they are doing."   *Luke 23:34*

REGRETS

How can I deal with regrets?

GOD'S RESPONSE

Purify me from my sins, and I will be clean; wash me, and I will be whiter than snow. . . . Don't keep looking at my sins. Remove the stain of my guilt.   *Psalm 51:7, 9*

Fear not; you will no longer live in shame. The shame of your youth and the sorrows of widowhood will be remembered no more.   *Isaiah 54:4*

Oh, what joy for those whose rebellion is forgiven, whose sin is put out of sight!   *Psalm 32:1*

R EGRETS FROM THE PAST can negatively affect every day of your life. Regret is often a sign that you cannot forgive yourself, or that you feel that you do not deserve forgiveness. However, in God's eyes, you are already forgiven; you just need to ask. He will help you forgive yourself and others and receive his forgiveness. Allow his forgiveness to bless you and free you from the guilt of regret.

GOD'S CHALLENGE

No, dear brothers and sisters, I am still not all I should be, but I am focusing all my energies on this one thing: Forgetting the past and looking forward to what lies ahead.   *Philippians 3:13*

LEGACY

How can I make lasting memories of God's work in my life?

GOD'S RESPONSE

We will use these stones to build a memorial. In the future, your children will ask, "What do these stones mean to you?" *Joshua 4:6*

A S THE ISRAELITES SET UP STONES to remind them of God's miraculous parting of the Jordan River, we can think of creative ways to remind ourselves and our families of God's special work in our lives and in the lives of those who went before us. We can celebrate special anniversaries, write spiritual journals, sing worship songs, or tell stories of memory-laden objects to remind us of God's blessing in our lives. We need reminders of God's faithfulness to us. What are you doing today to show God's faithfulness to future generations?

GOD'S PROMISE

God said, "I am giving you a sign as evidence of my eternal covenant with you and all living creatures. I have placed my rainbow in the clouds. It is the sign of my permanent promise to you and to all the earth." *Genesis 9:12-13*

EXAMPLE

In what ways can I be a good example?

GOD'S RESPONSE

You know that the way we lived among you was further proof of the truth of our message.   *1 Thessalonians 1:5*

You yourself must be an example to them by doing good deeds of every kind.   *Titus 2:7*

W HETHER YOU LIKE IT OR NOT, people are always watching you. This means that you are setting an example for others, good or bad. You can set a good example by living as closely as possible to Jesus' attitudes and actions. If you use Jesus as your example, you won't have to worry that you are setting a poor example for others. What kind of example have you been demonstrating to others lately?

GOD'S PROMISE

Be an example to all believers in what you teach, in the way you live, in your love, your faith, and your purity. . . . Stay true to what is right, and God will save you and those who hear you.   *1 Timothy 4:12, 16*

HYPOCRISY

How can I avoid being a hypocrite?

GOD'S RESPONSE

If you claim to be religious but don't control your tongue, you are just fooling yourself, and your religion is worthless. *James 1:26*

My dear brothers and sisters, how can you claim that you have faith in our glorious Lord Jesus Christ if you favor some people more than others? *James 2:1*

HYPOCRISY IS NOT PRACTICING what you preach. You claim to believe something, but your actions contradict this. Perhaps the worst hypocrisy is found in a Christian who claims to serve God but behaves as if he doesn't. The only sure way to avoid hypocrisy in your life is to faithfully serve God without contradiction. This involves continually studying God's Word so that you can avoid confusing God's standards of living with those of the world.

GOD'S PROMISE

False prophets and hypocrites—evil people who claim to want my advice—will all be punished for their sins. *Ezekiel 14:10*

WORK

What principles should guide my work?

GOD'S RESPONSE

Whatever you do, do well.   *Ecclesiastes 9:10*

Do not cheat or rob anyone. Always pay your hired workers promptly.   *Leviticus 19:13*

The LORD demands fairness in every business deal; he sets the standard.   *Proverbs 16:11*

G OOD WORK HONORS GOD and brings meaning and joy to your life. Emulate the character traits you see in God's work: excellence, concern for the well-being of others, purpose, beauty, and service. When you have the perspective that you are actually working for God, it takes the focus away from the task and onto why you are doing it—to help people know God. Then the excitement and high interest that come from doing your work for God are not primarily in the work, but from the one for whom you do the work.

GOD'S PROMISE

Use honest weights and measures, so that you will enjoy a long life in the land the LORD your God is giving you. Those who cheat with dishonest weights and measures are detestable to the LORD your God. *Deuteronomy 25:15-16*

WORK

How is my work important to the Lord?

GOD'S RESPONSE

Work hard, but not just to please your masters when they are watching. . . . Work with enthusiasm, as though you were working for the Lord rather than for people. *Ephesians 6:6-7*

If your gift is to encourage others, do it! If you have money, share it generously. If God has given you leadership ability, take the responsibility seriously. And if you have a gift for showing kindness to others, do it gladly. *Romans 12:8*

WORK IS AN IMPORTANT PART of God's plan for your life. God created work to give us purpose. He gave Adam work to do in the Garden of Eden before sin entered the world (Genesis 2:15). God promises three kinds of rewards for faithful work: (1) having a more credible witness to nonbelievers; (2) having our needs met without having to depend financially on others; and (3) fulfilling our God-given purpose. When you work diligently, you experience many benefits that you can pass on to others.

GOD'S CHALLENGE

To enjoy your work and accept your lot in life—that is indeed a gift from God. *Ecclesiastes 5:19*

WORK

What if my work has nothing to do with anything "Christian"—how can God be glorified in my work?

GOD'S RESPONSE

Having finished his task, God rested from all his work. . . . The LORD God placed the man in the Garden of Eden to tend and care for it.   *Genesis 2:2, 15*

We worked hard day and night so that we would not be a burden to any of you.   *2 Thessalonians 3:8*

T HE INTRINSIC VALUE OF WORK is anchored in God's character. Part of being made in his image is sharing the industrious and creative aspects of his nature. Christians are needed in all kinds of vocations. Whatever your job, believe that God has placed you there for a reason, and then do your work well as a service to God and as a way to show others his love in action through you.

GOD'S PROMISE

This should be your ambition: to live a quiet life, minding your own business and working with your hands, just as we commanded you before. As a result, people who are not Christians will respect the way you live, and you will not need to depend on others to meet your financial needs.   *1 Thessalonians 4:11-12*

INTEGRITY

What principles should guide how I conduct my business?

GOD'S RESPONSE

Do not cheat or rob anyone. Always pay your hired workers promptly.   *Leviticus 19:13*

The LORD demands fairness in every business deal; he sets the standard.   *Proverbs 16:11*

TREAT OTHERS AS YOU WOULD want them to treat you, with honesty and fairness in all your dealings. You should not ask, Am I getting everything I can get out of this deal? Instead ask, Is this deal fair for both parties? That attitude does not go over well in many businesses today, but the alternative is to compromise your integrity. What is the personal cost to you if you do that? Almost anything is easier to restore than the value of damaged integrity.

GOD'S CHALLENGE

People with integrity have firm footing, but those who follow crooked paths will slip and fall.   *Proverbs 10:9*

BUSINESS

Is God interested in the success of my business?

GOD'S RESPONSE

A Jew named Aquila . . . had recently arrived from Italy with his wife, Priscilla. . . . Paul lived and worked with them, for they were tentmakers just as he was.   *Acts 18:2-3*

You know that these hands of mine have worked to pay my own way, and I have even supplied the needs of those who were with me.   *Acts 20:34*

PAUL, AQUILA, AND PRISCILLA WERE all Christian leaders in ministry and in business. They are examples of early Christians who used their business and some of its proceeds to serve God. God honors integrity, excellence, and hard work. While these character traits don't necessarily bring financial blessing, you can be sure that God will take special interest in any enterprise whose leaders acknowledge him and faithfully live by his standards. The impact of your business will be far more significant than a strong balance sheet.

GOD'S PROMISE

Work hard and cheerfully at whatever you do, as though you were working for the Lord rather than for people. . . . The Lord will give you an inheritance as your reward. *Colossians 3:23-24*

SUPERVISION

How should I treat the people who report to me?

GOD'S RESPONSE

Never take advantage of poor laborers. . . . Pay them their wages. . . . Otherwise they might cry out to the LORD against you, and it would be counted against you as sin. *Deuteronomy 24:14-15*

Boaz arrived from Bethlehem and greeted the harvesters. "The LORD be with you!" he said. "The LORD bless you!" the harvesters replied.   *Ruth 2:4*

G OD EXPECTS YOU TO HOLD YOURSELF to higher standards than those you require of your workers. Never take advantage of your employees. Pay them fairly and promptly. Encourage your workers. Thank them for jobs well done. Never lead through intimidation. Apologize when you are wrong. In short, treat your employees as you would want to be treated. Though you fulfill different roles in business, you are all equals before God.

GOD'S CHALLENGE

Do for others what you would like them to do for you. *Matthew 7:12*

EMPLOYEES

How can I foster a good relationship with my boss?

GOD'S RESPONSE

Unless you are faithful in small matters, you won't be faithful in large ones.   *Luke 16:10*

Faithful messengers are as refreshing as snow in the heat of summer. They revive the spirit of their employer. *Proverbs 25:13*

Lazy people are a pain to their employer. They are like smoke in the eyes or vinegar that sets the teeth on edge. *Proverbs 10:26*

Y OU SHOULD BE FAITHFUL and honest in every aspect of your work, for when you can be trusted with small things you have a better chance of being trusted with larger responsibilities. Try to foster a work environment that your boss can be proud of. If your boss is critical and overbearing, continue to work hard and display a cheerful spirit. Others will notice and your reputation will be enhanced. Perhaps the most important question to ask is whether your coworkers would believe you if you told them you were a Christian.

GOD'S PROMISE

Workers who protect their employer's interests will be rewarded.   *Proverbs 27:18*

COMPETITION

Can competition be constructive?

GOD'S RESPONSE

Whatever I am now, it is all because God poured out his special favor on me—and not without results. For I have worked harder than all the other apostles, yet it was not I but God who was working through me by his grace. *1 Corinthians 15:10*

"MOVE UP OR MOVE OVER." "Winning isn't everything; it's the only thing." These are the slogans of a world driven by competition. Competition can be destructive when infected with selfish ambition and sinful pride. It destroys relationships because it hardens your heart toward fairness and compassion. But when properly focused, competition can drive us to improve ourselves and sharpen our skills. The apostle Paul was competitive and God used his verbal and organizational skills to reach enormous numbers of people for Jesus while establishing churches throughout the world. Competition should bring out the best in you, not the worst.

GOD'S CHALLENGE

Remember that in a race everyone runs, but only one person gets the prize. You also must run in such a way that you will win. *1 Corinthians 9:24*

COMPETITION

When does competition become a bad thing?

GOD'S RESPONSE

The proud Pharisee stood by himself and prayed this prayer: "I thank you, God, that I am not a sinner like everyone else, especially like that tax collector over there! For I never cheat, I don't sin, I don't commit adultery."   *Luke 18:11*

The disciples came to Jesus and asked, "Which of us is greatest in the Kingdom of Heaven?" . . . Then [Jesus] said, . . . "Anyone who becomes as humble as this little child is the greatest in the Kingdom of Heaven." *Matthew 18:1, 3-4*

COMPETITION CAN BE A FOOTHOLD for pride and jealousy because it leads you to compare yourself with others. Everyone has equal worth in God's eyes; any time you begin to think of yourself as more important or better than others, your competitive spirit is taking you in the wrong direction. When humility fuels your competitive nature you give everything you have to service, not to self.

GOD'S CHALLENGE

Follow the Lord's rules for doing his work, just as an athlete either follows the rules or is disqualified and wins no prize.   *2 Timothy 2:5*

COMPARISONS

How can I stop comparing myself to others?

GOD'S RESPONSE

When others are happy, be happy with them. If they are sad, share their sorrow.   *Romans 12:15*

Why do you condemn another Christian? Why do you look down on another Christian? Remember, each of us will stand personally before the judgment seat of God. . . . Yes, each of us will have to give a personal account to God.   *Romans 14:10, 12*

L ET'S FACE IT. Most of the time we compare ourselves to others to convince ourselves that we are better looking, smarter, more skilled, or better off. This puts the focus on ourselves. Instead, put yourself in the other person's shoes and attempt to feel as they do. That way, when they succeed, you can genuinely celebrate with them and when they fail, you can empathize. Remember, we are all worthy because Jesus paid a high price for us.

GOD'S PROMISE

How precious are your thoughts about me, O God! They are innumerable!   *Psalm 139:17*

ASSUMPTIONS

*What happens when we jump
to the wrong conclusions?*

GOD'S RESPONSE

"But Lord," exclaimed Ananias, "I've heard about the terrible things this man has done to the believers in Jerusalem!" . . . But the Lord said, . . . "Saul is my chosen instrument to take my message to the Gentiles and to kings, as well as to the people of Israel."   *Acts 9:13, 15*

JUMPING TO THE WRONG CONCLUSIONS (also known as prejudice) leads only to fear and worry about what will happen next. Jumping to conclusions assumes that the worst option will happen. With the God of the universe on your side, shouldn't you consider his helping hand as the best available option?

GOD'S CHALLENGE

Be careful not to jump to conclusions before the Lord returns as to whether or not someone is faithful. When the Lord comes, he will bring our deepest secrets to light and will reveal our private motives.   *1 Corinthians 4:5*

RESPONSIBILITY

What is a responsible person like?

GOD'S RESPONSE

Potiphar . . . put Joseph in charge of his entire household and entrusted him with all his business dealings. . . . With Joseph there, he didn't have a worry in the world. *Genesis 39:4, 6*

E VEN AS A SLAVE, Joseph was put in charge of Potiphar's entire household. When Joseph was thrown into prison, the warden put him in charge of the other prisoners. Both Potiphar and the warden saw that Joseph was clearly a responsible person. Responsibility means being able to discern what needs to be done and following through to see that it happens. It means being dependable and consistent in word, attitude, and deed. Christians should be more responsible than most because they have a higher calling to display a godly character at work and in relationships (Colossians 3:23-24). How you handle responsibility determines whether you will be trusted with more.

GOD'S CHALLENGE

To those who use well what they are given, even more will be given, and they will have an abundance. But from those who are unfaithful, even what little they have will be taken away. *Matthew 25:29*

FATHER

*How can I draw close to God
as my heavenly Father?*

GOD'S RESPONSE

We know that there is only one God, the Father, who created everything, and we exist for him. And there is only one Lord, Jesus Christ, through whom God made everything and through whom we have been given life. *1 Corinthians 8:6*

A GOOD FATHER LOVES HIS CHILDREN by spending time with them, providing for them, protecting them, celebrating with them, disciplining them, praying with them, teaching them right from wrong, and leading them to faith in Jesus Christ. God is the perfect father, and he always will be. Earthly fathers sometimes let us down and eventually they leave this earth, but God will never disappoint you. His love is everlasting and he longs to draw close to you. Let him do so, and you will experience a peace like never before.

GOD'S PROMISE

Because you Gentiles have become his children, God has sent the Spirit of his Son into your hearts, and now you can call God your dear Father.   *Galatians 4:6*

POWER

How does God show his power?

GOD'S RESPONSE

I will come like a lion from the thickets of the Jordan, leaping on the sheep in the pasture. I will chase Edom from its land, and I will appoint the leader of my choice. For who is like me, and who can challenge me? What ruler can oppose my will? *Jeremiah 49:19*

The Sovereign LORD has spoken—I dare not refuse to proclaim his message! *Amos 3:8*

ONE OF THE DESCRIPTIONS OF GOD in the Bible is as the Lion of Judah, a fierce fighter on behalf of his people. He is the God who created all things, the God of lightning and thunder. He has flooded the entire earth, blinded whole armies, and rained burning sulfur from the sky against those who opposed him and his people. But God uses this same power to come to the aid of his people who declare their faith and loyalty in him. If you are under attack from the enemy, call upon God's mighty power to rescue you.

GOD'S PROMISE

Someday the people will follow the LORD. I will roar like a lion, and my people will return trembling from the west. *Hosea 11:10*

WARRIOR GOD

In what ways does God do battle for me?

GOD'S RESPONSE

The LORD will march forth like a mighty man; he will come out like a warrior, full of fury. He will shout his thundering battle cry, and he will crush all his enemies.   *Isaiah 42:13*

This is what the LORD says: Do not be afraid! Don't be discouraged by this mighty army, for the battle is not yours, but God's.   *2 Chronicles 20:15*

T HE PURPOSE OF EVIL IS TO DEFY GOD and to wear down believers until they are led into sin. This pleases Satan and gives him greater power over the earth. But God is a warrior. A battle rages in the spiritual realm and, as a believer, you are right in the thick of it. God is always ready to fight on your behalf, always ready to come to your defense. In addition, he provides you with armor so that you can fight alongside him (Ephesians 6:11-18). But you must join God in the battle or you will be vulnerable and helpless to withstand the enemy. If you join, you are guaranteed victory.

GOD'S PROMISE

The whole world has now become the Kingdom of our Lord and of his Christ, and he will reign forever and ever. *Revelation 11:15*

RESCUER

Will God rescue me even when my troubles are my own fault?

GOD'S RESPONSE

Don't be afraid. Just stand where you are and watch the LORD rescue you.   *Exodus 14:13*

Stand still and watch the LORD's victory.   *2 Chronicles 20:17*

Stand here and see the great thing the LORD is about to do.
1 Samuel 12:16

G OD OFTEN ALLOWS THE CONSEQUENCES of sin to take their course, even for believers, because he cares about them. God uses those consequences to remind you of the danger of sin, to encourage you to work hard to avoid it, and to prepare you to face other troubles in the future. He cares for you so deeply that he will use even your self-made troubles to discipline you. For any of these tough circumstances there is reason to praise God: He redeems our mistakes, he teaches us wisdom through adversity, and he promises to help us through tough times.

GOD'S PROMISE

He rescues me and keeps me safe from the battle
waged against me, even though many still oppose me.
Psalm 55:18

SUFFERING

Why do bad things happen to good people?

GOD'S RESPONSE

I was kidnapped from my homeland . . . and now I'm here in jail, but I did nothing to deserve it.   *Genesis 40:15*

Job replied, . . . "Should we accept only good things from the hand of God and never anything bad?"   *Job 2:10*

S OMETIMES THE SUFFERING THAT COMES to you is not your fault. It just happens. When it does, how you react to the suffering is critical. The Lord was with Joseph and blessed him, and yet Joseph was in prison through no fault of his own. God does not want to see you suffer, but we live in a fallen world where sin is often allowed to run its course, affecting both believers and nonbelievers. Although God doesn't want you to suffer, he often brings renewal, healing, and spiritual maturity through suffering so that you can be stronger and better equipped to help others.

GOD'S PROMISE

Though he brings grief, he also shows compassion according to the greatness of his unfailing love. For he does not enjoy hurting people or causing them sorrow. *Lamentations 3:32-33*

GIANTS

*What can I do when I'm surrounded
by giant problems?*

GOD'S RESPONSE

Today the LORD will conquer you . . . and the whole world
will know that there is a God in Israel! And everyone will
know that the LORD does not need weapons to rescue his
people. It is his battle, not ours. The LORD will give you
to us!   *1 Samuel 17:46-47*

THE STORY OF DAVID AND GOLIATH has a theme of reality vs. distortion. The reality was that God had promised that his people would not lose their land if they followed
him. The distortion was the large giant that seemed more
real and immediate than God's promise and presence. Fear
can distort your view of reality and paralyze you. The giants
in your path can appear more powerful than your Almighty
God who promises to deliver you if you let him fight for
you. Sooner or later you will face some kind of fearsome
giant—an especially great temptation, guilt, sin, anger, anxi-
ety, depression, disease, or other difficulty. Don't let the size
of the giant reduce your awareness of the size of your God!

GOD'S PROMISE

Overwhelming victory is ours through Christ,
who loved us.   *Romans 8:37*

GOD'S JUDGMENT

Should I be afraid of facing God's judgment?

GOD'S RESPONSE

He will judge the world with justice and rule the nations with fairness.   *Psalm 9:8*

Everyone's work will be put through the fire to see whether or not it keeps its value.   *1 Corinthians 3:13*

THE FINAL EVENT OF HISTORY is a twofold judgment. First, God will judge all people who have ever lived to determine whether they should enter heaven or hell—based solely on their allegiance to and faith in God. This is the judgment to fear if you have not accepted Jesus Christ as your Savior and asked him to forgive your sins. Second, God will judge the deeds of all who enter heaven and give rewards accordingly. This second judgment does not determine whether or not you get into heaven, but what rewards you receive when you get there. How do you think you will be judged?

GOD'S PROMISE

For God so loved the world that he gave his only Son, so that everyone who believes in him will not perish but have eternal life.   *John 3:16*

COMPLAINING

When things get stressful I have the tendency to complain. Is that wrong?

GOD'S RESPONSE

The people of Israel also began to complain. "Oh, for some meat!" they exclaimed. . . . "Day after day we have nothing to eat but this manna!"   *Numbers 11:4, 6*

In everything you do, stay away from complaining and arguing, so that no one can speak a word of blame against you.   *Philippians 2:14-15*

COMPLAINING IS A COMMON RESPONSE to stress that allows you to express your frustrations; however, it is not the right way to make yourself feel better. God calls complaining a sin because it is self-centered. You didn't get what you wanted, you got less than someone else, or you think you didn't get what you deserved. The focus is on yourself. The solution is to be grateful for what you do have instead of focusing on what you don't have.

GOD'S CHALLENGE

Let everything you say be good and helpful, so that your words will be an encouragement to those who hear them. *Ephesians 4:29*

COMPROMISE

How do we live in today's culture without compromising our convictions?

GOD'S RESPONSE

Daniel made up his mind not to defile himself by eating the food. . . . He asked . . . permission to eat other things instead . . . and [suggested] ten days on a diet of vegetables and water. . . . At the end of the ten days, Daniel . . . looked healthier and better nourished than the young men who had been eating the food assigned by the king.   *Daniel 1:8, 12, 15*

T HERE IS A TIME TO COMPROMISE and a time not to compromise. When the forces of evil want their way, you cannot budge. To compromise God's truth, God's ways, or God's Word is to negotiate with that which is unholy. The test of acceptable compromise is simple: Can an agreement be reached that satisfies both parties without anyone's morals being sacrificed? To give up godliness for anything is a bad bargain. You lose and Satan wins.

GOD'S CHALLENGE

Put on all of God's armor so that you will be able to stand firm against all strategies and tricks of the Devil. *Ephesians 6:11*

REBELLION

*Isn't a certain amount of rebellion to be expected—
for example, from teenagers?*

GOD'S RESPONSE

This younger son . . . wasted all his money on wild living.
. . . When he finally came to his senses, he said to himself,
. . . "I will go home to my father and say, 'Father, I have
sinned against both heaven and you.'" . . . And while he was
still a long distance away, his father saw him coming. Filled
with love and compassion, he ran to his son, embraced
him, and kissed him.   *Luke 15:13, 17-18, 20*

THE STORY OF THE PRODIGAL SON is a classic, heart-
breaking story of the rebellion of a son against his
father. Yes, rebellion is to be expected because all people
have a sinful nature. Haven't we all rebelled against God?
And too often, we are slow to forgive when the rebellious one realizes what he has done. We should take the
example of the prodigal's father and continue to love
rebellious people until they come to their senses, then
welcome them back with open arms.

GOD'S PROMISE

Once again you will have compassion on us. You will
trample our sins under your feet and throw them into
the depths of the ocean!   *Micah 7:19*

PLANS

If God has a plan, why should we plan?

GOD'S RESPONSE

Joseph's suggestions were well received by Pharaoh and his advisers. As they discussed who should be appointed for the job, Pharaoh said, "Who could do it better than Joseph? For he is a man who is obviously filled with the spirit of God." *Genesis 41:37-38*

J OSEPH'S WILLINGNESS TO USE his gifts to help the Egyptians plan for seven years of famine allowed God's plan to be fulfilled. While asking God to bless our plans, we should be willing to use our gifts and abilities to join him in his plans. What a privilege when God uses us in the implementation of his intentions! How do you know what plans God wants you to be a part of? The first step, like Joseph, is to have an open mind and an obedient heart. The path of obedience will always take you in the right direction. Plan to become part of God's plan.

GOD'S PROMISE

Trust in the LORD with all your heart; do not depend on your own understanding. Seek his will in all you do, and he will direct your paths. *Proverbs 3:5-6*

FRIENDSHIP

How can I be God's friend?

GOD'S RESPONSE

The LORD replied to Moses, "I will indeed do what you have asked, for you have found favor with me, and you are my friend."   *Exodus 33:17*

Friendship with the LORD is reserved for those who fear him.   *Psalm 25:14*

THINK OF THE QUALITIES YOU look for in a friend. Perhaps you would list honesty, loyalty, or availability. God desires these same qualities from you as his friend. He wants you to come to him honestly with your struggles and successes, to remain faithful and loyal to him and his Word, and to make yourself available to spend quality time with him. You fear separation from your friends—how much more should you fear separation from God? Respect him, honor him, and remain loyal to him; he will call you his friend.

GOD'S PROMISE

I no longer call you servants, because a master doesn't confide in his servants. Now you are my friends, since I have told you everything the Father told me.   *John 15:15*

FRIENDSHIP

*How can I keep God at the center of my
other friendships?*

GOD'S RESPONSE

Love is patient and kind. Love is not jealous. . . . Love
does not demand its own way.   *1 Corinthians 13:4-5*

A friend is always loyal, and a brother is born to help in
time of need.   *Proverbs 17:17*

Don't team up with those who are unbelievers. How can
goodness be a partner with wickedness? How can light
live with darkness?   *2 Corinthians 6:14*

P AUL'S TIMELESS DESCRIPTION of Christian love should
apply in all your friendships. To be a good friend, be
loyal, helpful, kind, and forgiving. True friendships are
glued together with bonds of loyalty and commitment.
They remain intact despite changing external circumstances. If you demonstrate to your friends all the characteristics that God demonstrates to you, you will always
have strong and loyal friends.

GOD'S PROMISE

[Jesus said,] "Where two or three gather together because
they are mine, I am there among them."   *Matthew 18:20*

FRIENDSHIP

Is it possible to have close male friendships?

GOD'S RESPONSE

After David had finished talking with Saul, he met Jonathan, the king's son. There was an immediate bond of love between them, and they became the best of friends. . . . And Jonathan made a special vow to be David's friend, and he sealed the pact by giving him his robe, tunic, sword, bow, and belt.   *1 Samuel 18:1, 3-4*

IT IS POSSIBLE TO HAVE CLOSE FRIENDSHIPS with other men—in fact, it is vital. Men have issues and struggles that women may have a hard time understanding (and vice versa). It is important to know other men who understand these issues and feel comfortable enough to talk about them with you. If you are having trouble knowing where to find close friendships with other men, try looking for a men's accountability group or a Bible study in a local church.

GOD'S PROMISE

As iron sharpens iron, a friend sharpens a friend.
Proverbs 27:17

FRIENDSHIP

Does the Bible offer guidelines for men's friendships with women?

GOD'S RESPONSE

Let there be no sexual immorality, impurity, or greed among you. Such sins have no place among God's people. Obscene stories, foolish talk, and coarse jokes—these are not for you. Instead, let there be thankfulness to God. . . . Be careful how you live, not as fools but as those who are wise.   *Ephesians 5:3-4, 15*

F RIENDSHIPS WITH WOMEN are an important part of most men's lives—but also a powerful source of temptation. Healthy relationships with women are appropriate. Jesus had many female friends, some of whom even traveled with him from time to time (see Luke 8:1-3). But a married man must be careful to ensure that friendship with a woman doesn't lead to inappropriate emotional intimacy and betray the trust and commitment he shares with his wife. Here are three ways to safeguard yourself: Never be alone with a woman who is not your wife; avoid talking with women about your marriage; always treat women with great respect.

GOD'S PROMISE

God blesses those whose hearts are pure, for they will see God.   *Matthew 5:8*

FRIENDSHIP

A lot of my friends are not Christians.
How can I be a good friend to them?

GOD'S RESPONSE

I, the Son of Man, feast and drink, and you say, "He's a glutton and a drunkard, and a friend of the worst sort of sinners!" *Matthew 11:19*

You are the light of the world—like a city on a mountain, glowing in the night for all to see. Don't hide your light under a basket! Instead, put it on a stand and let it shine for all. *Matthew 5:14-15*

JESUS GAVE YOU AN EXAMPLE by how he lived. He didn't avoid unbelievers; instead, he made friends with them and sought their company. He did this to influence them with the love of God. Don't condemn your friends that do not believe. Instead, encourage them with the strength and commitment you display through Christ. You can learn a lot from them without being influenced to follow lifestyle choices that are contrary to God's ways.

GOD'S CHALLENGE

Be kind to each other, tenderhearted, forgiving one another, just as God through Christ has forgiven you. *Ephesians 4:32*

CONSCIENCE

What is the danger of ignoring my conscience?

GOD'S RESPONSE

For the truth about God is known to them instinctively. God has put this knowledge in their hearts. *Romans 1:19*

Cling tightly to your faith in Christ, and always keep your conscience clear. For some people have deliberately violated their consciences; as a result, their faith has been shipwrecked. *1 Timothy 1:19*

YOUR CONSCIENCE IS A GIFT from God, an instinct he has placed inside you that makes you aware of your sins and gives you an appropriate sense of guilt and shame. It then calls you to act by righting the wrong and receiving forgiveness from God and others. Ignoring your conscience dulls it and allows sin's consequences to grow unchecked without your feeling bad about it. This is like ignoring warning lights at a railroad crossing when a freight train is barreling down on you.

GOD'S CHALLENGE

My conscience is clear, but that isn't what matters. It is the Lord himself who will examine me and decide. *1 Corinthians 4:4*

REST

What is God's prescription for my fatigue?

GOD'S RESPONSE

On the seventh day, having finished his task, God rested from all his work. And God blessed the seventh day and declared it holy, because it was the day when he rested from his work of creation. *Genesis 2:2-3*

It is useless for you to work so hard from early morning until late at night, anxiously working for food to eat; for God gives rest to his loved ones. *Psalm 127:2*

Jesus said, "Let's get away from the crowds for a while and rest." *Mark 6:31*

G OD WANTS YOU TO TAKE A BREAK and get some rest. He set aside a full day of rest after Creation as an example for us to follow. Jesus understood the needs and limitations of his disciples and took them away for a break. Work is good, but it must be balanced by regular attention to the health of your body, mind, soul, and spirit. Whole life comes from holy rest.

GOD'S CHALLENGE

Keep my Sabbath days of rest and show reverence toward my sanctuary, for I am the LORD. *Leviticus 19:30*

REST

Can I experience true refreshment in my times of rest?

GOD'S RESPONSE

It is a permanent sign of my covenant with them. For in six days the LORD made heaven and earth, but he rested on the seventh day and was refreshed.   *Exodus 31:17*

The LORD replied, "I will personally go with you, Moses. I will give you rest—everything will be fine for you." *Exodus 33:14*

I lay down and slept. I woke up in safety, for the LORD was watching over me.   *Psalm 3:5*

R EST IS ONLY REFRESHING when you truly set aside your work and your worries. Rest is physically, mentally, and psychologically refreshing; a healthy body, mind, and emotions make us more productive. Rest is also spiritually refreshing; a healthy soul allows us to fully focus on God. Above all, rest reminds us that we depend on God's provision, not on our own efforts.

GOD'S PROMISE

God gives rest to his loved ones.   *Psalm 127:2*

PRAYER

How can I pray for my country?

GOD'S RESPONSE

I urge you, first of all, to pray for all people. As you make your requests, plead for God's mercy upon them, and give thanks. Pray this way for kings and all others who are in authority, so that we can live in peace and quietness, in godliness and dignity.   *1 Timothy 2:1-2*

PRAY FOR YOUR NATION. Pray that it will be protected by God's mighty hand. Pray for your leaders to be humble and wise, able to discern right from wrong, and to be champions of the needy and helpless. A nation that condones and endorses immorality is subject to judgment and will eventually collapse from the inside out. A nation that collectively worships the one true God will stand firm.

GOD'S PROMISE

If my people who are called by my name will humble themselves and pray and seek my face and turn from their wicked ways, I will hear from heaven and will forgive their sins and heal their land.   *2 Chronicles 7:14*

LEADERS

What if the leaders of my country leave something to be desired? How do I respond?

GOD'S RESPONSE

Obey the government, for God is the one who put it there. All governments have been placed in power by God. So those who refuse to obey the laws of the land are refusing to obey God, and punishment will follow.   *Romans 13:1-2*

W E MUST BE RESPONSIBLE CITIZENS as well as responsible Christians. Every government is in power because God allows it to be. Therefore, you should work hard to obey the laws of the land. The Bible is also clear that you should never violate God's moral standards. This means that you should never allow the government to force you to disobey God. You should not disobey the government for personal reasons, but only for moral reasons when God's laws are violated. Civil disobedience comes with a price, so if you are compelled to disobey, you must be courageous enough to accept the consequences.

GOD'S PROMISE

If you keep looking steadily into God's perfect law—the law that sets you free—and if you do what it says and don't forget what you heard, then God will bless you for doing it.   *James 1:25*

FREEDOM

What does it mean to be free in Christ?
What does that freedom look like?

GOD'S RESPONSE

You are not slaves; you are free. But your freedom is not an excuse to do evil. You are free to live as God's slaves.
1 Peter 2:16

Christ has really set us free. Now make sure that you stay free, and don't get tied up again in slavery to the law.
Galatians 5:1

The Lord is the Spirit, and wherever the Spirit of the Lord is, he gives freedom.   *2 Corinthians 3:17*

FREEDOM IN CHRIST MEANS FREEDOM from all the things in life that bring you down—guilt, slavery to sin, fear, and addiction. But this does not operate in a vacuum; you are free to do other things—free to follow Christ, free to let go of self and worship God, free to live by the truth of God's Word, and free to serve him wholeheartedly.

GOD'S PROMISE

You will know the truth, and the truth will set you free. . . . So if the Son sets you free, you will indeed be free.
John 8:32, 36

WEARINESS

What can help me when I am weary or discouraged?

GOD'S RESPONSE

Happy are those who are strong in the LORD, who set their minds on a pilgrimage to Jerusalem. When they walk through the Valley of Weeping, it will become a place of refreshing springs, where pools of blessing collect after the rains! They will continue to grow stronger, and each of them will appear before God in Jerusalem. *Psalm 84:5-7*

OCCASIONALLY, YOU NEED REFRESHMENT to renew your soul, your mind, and your body. Refreshment comes from spending time alone with God in prayer, reading his Word, listening for his voice, and reflecting on your blessings. Refreshment comes by disciplining yourself to get enough sleep and to eat well. And it comes from fellowship with other believers who are encouragers rather than complainers. Follow this prescription and you will have a new outlook on life.

GOD'S PROMISE

Don't get tired of doing what is good. Don't get discouraged and give up, for we will reap a harvest of blessing at the appropriate time. *Galatians 6:9*

STRENGTH

Can God use me when I feel useless?

GOD'S RESPONSE

Moses pleaded with the LORD, "O LORD, I'm just not a good speaker. . . . I'm clumsy with words."

"Who makes mouths?" the LORD asked him. . . . "I will help you speak well, and I will tell you what to say." *Exodus 4:10-12*

Elijah was afraid and fled for his life. . . . He sat down under a solitary broom tree and prayed that he might die. "I have had enough, LORD," he said. "Take my life." . . . But as he was sleeping, an angel touched him and told him, "Get up and eat!" *1 Kings 19:3-5*

THERE ARE NO LIMITS TO WHAT GOD CAN do in and through you. In his strength you have power to do things you could never do on your own. In fact, God delights in taking your inadequacies and using them for his service. Then it is obvious to all that God is working through you. Your weaknesses, given humbly to God, are great tools in his hands.

GOD'S PROMISE

I can do everything with the help of Christ who gives me the strength I need. *Philippians 4:13*

NEIGHBOR

How am I to love my neighbor?

GOD'S RESPONSE

Love your neighbor as yourself.   *Leviticus 19:18*

"Which of these three would you say was a neighbor to the man who was attacked by bandits?" Jesus asked.

The man replied, "The one who showed him mercy."

Then Jesus said, "Yes, now go and do the same." *Luke 10:36-37*

JESUS SAID TO LOVE YOUR NEIGHBOR as yourself is the second greatest commandment. Why do both the Old Testament and Jesus say to love your neighbor as yourself? Because God knows that our first instinct is to take care of ourselves. We can train ourselves to give the needs of others equal priority with our own, and this is what love is all about. If we truly love others the way God intended, we will naturally carry out all of God's other instructions for service. Love directed inward has nowhere else to go. Love directed outward can change the world one person at a time.

GOD'S CHALLENGE

It is good when you truly obey our Lord's royal command found in the Scriptures: "Love your neighbor as yourself." *James 2:8*

REFRESHMENT

In what ways can my mind be refreshed?

GOD'S RESPONSE

I will put my laws in their minds so they will understand them, and I will write them on their hearts so they will obey them.   *Hebrews 8:10*

I have tried to stimulate your wholesome thinking and refresh your memory. I want you to remember and understand what the holy prophets said long ago and what our Lord and Savior commanded through your apostles.
2 Peter 3:1-2

Y OUR MIND IS REFRESHED WHEN YOU READ the Bible and allow the words of God to calm you, encourage you, and heal you. Then you are prepared to let the Holy Spirit change the way you think. Let God's wonderful promises refresh your gratitude as you remember all he has done for you and refresh your hope as you anticipate all that he promises to do for you.

GOD'S CHALLENGE

Those who are dominated by the sinful nature think about sinful things, but those who are controlled by the Holy Spirit think about things that please the Spirit.
Romans 8:5

SUPERSTITION

How am I superstitious?

GOD'S RESPONSE

[Balak said,] "Please come and curse these people for me because they are too powerful for me."
Numbers 22:6 (NLT2)

BALAK, THE MOABITE KING, had a problem too big for him to solve. A mighty army was camping in his land. His only hope, he believed, was to invoke a curse on the Israelites. Because he didn't know God, magic was his only higher power. So he called for Balaam, a man with an international reputation for sorcery. When we need help, too often we look first for some magical solution. "Good luck," our friends tell us. "I hope things work out," they say, as if our lives are left to chance. Sometimes we even repeat superstitious acts that seemed to work the last time we needed help. But what about prayer? Shouldn't we go straight to God, who tells us that he will not ignore those who cry to him for help? Don't follow Balak's example; he tapped into the wrong power source.

GOD'S PROMISE

The LORD is close to all who call on him, yes, to all who call on him sincerely.   *Psalm 145:18*

PLEASURE

Some seem to think that pleasure and the Christian life don't mix. Is that true?

GOD'S RESPONSE

I decided there is nothing better than to enjoy food and drink and to find satisfaction in work. Then I realized that this pleasure is from the hand of God.   *Ecclesiastes 2:24*

Oh, how delightful you are, my beloved; how pleasant for utter delight!   *Song of Songs 7:6*

The father of godly children has cause for joy. What a pleasure it is to have wise children.   *Proverbs 23:24*

GOD CREATED A BEAUTIFUL WORLD for you to enjoy. He gave you food and drink to refresh you and meaningful work for you to do. He gave you a family in which to take pleasure. In fact, he has abundantly given you all things to enjoy. God is pleased when you take pleasure in the gifts he has given you. Enjoying the gifts God gives us shows him that we are grateful for his generosity and kindness.

GOD'S CHALLENGE

Since everything God created is good, we should not reject any of it. We may receive it gladly, with thankful hearts. For we know it is made holy by the word of God and prayer.   *1 Timothy 4:4-5*

PLEASING GOD

In what ways can I give God pleasure?

GOD'S RESPONSE

The one who sent me is with me—he has not deserted me. For I always do those things that are pleasing to him. *John 8:29*

It was by faith that Enoch was taken up to heaven without dying. . . . But before he was taken up, he was approved as pleasing to God. So, you see, it is impossible to please God without faith. Anyone who wants to come to him must believe that there is a God and that he rewards those who sincerely seek him.   *Hebrews 11:5-6*

PART OF THE WAY WE PLEASE GOD is by obeying the instructions found in his Word. God's laws are not designed to burden people or to stifle their fun, but to free them to enjoy life in security and safety. Obeying God protects us from evil, leads us on right paths where we will find blessing, and directs us into service that will please him.

GOD'S PROMISE

His unchanging plan has always been to adopt us into his own family by bringing us to himself through Jesus Christ. And this gave him great pleasure.   *Ephesians 1:5*

DELIGHT

What does it mean that God delights in me?

GOD'S RESPONSE

The LORD your God will delight in you if you obey his voice and keep the commands and laws written in this Book of the Law, and if you turn to the LORD your God with all your heart and soul.   *Deuteronomy 30:10*

The LORD . . . delights in honesty.   *Proverbs 11:1*

The LORD . . . delights in those who have integrity. *Proverbs 11:20*

The LORD . . . delights in the prayers of the upright. *Proverbs 15:8*

C AN YOU—A FINITE, SINFUL HUMAN BEING—bring delight to the Lord, the creator of the universe? Yes, and it isn't that difficult, for he loves to delight in you. When you honor him, obey him, respond to his love, seek his forgiveness, and walk daily with him, you are giving him gifts, each of which he loves. Find ways that you can delight the Lord today.

GOD'S PROMISE

The LORD delights in his people; he crowns the humble with salvation.   *Psalm 149:4*

HAPPINESS

Will God give me real, lasting happiness?

GOD'S RESPONSE

O Lord Almighty, happy are those who trust in you. *Psalm 84:12*

Happy are those who obey his decrees and search for him with all their hearts. *Psalm 119:2*

Happy are those who fear the Lord. Yes, happy are those who delight in doing what he commands. *Psalm 112:1*

W E ARE HAPPY WHEN A TOOL—a power drill or laser level—works the way it was intended to work. This feeling of being happy, however, is just a shadow of the lasting happiness we experience when we function in the ways that God intended when he made us. We were created to live and to relate to others in certain ways that are clearly described in the Bible. When we follow these guidelines, we have the greatest possible impact on our present and on our future; we achieve our purpose; and we find true, lasting happiness.

GOD'S PROMISE

The godly can look forward to happiness. *Proverbs 11:23*

ABUNDANCE

*What is the abundance that God wants me
to experience?*

GOD'S RESPONSE

May you experience the love of Christ, though it is so great
you will never fully understand it. Then you will be filled
with the fullness of life and power that comes from God.
Ephesians 3:19

May you overflow with hope through the power of the
Holy Spirit.   *Romans 15:13*

TOO OFTEN WE DEFINE ABUNDANCE quantitatively by
how many possessions or how much financial wealth
we have. Instead, we should think of abundance as God
does—as the marvelous gift of salvation and eternal life;
the blessings of a relationship with the creator of the
universe; the treasure of God's Word; and the wonderful
character traits of godliness, truthfulness, wisdom, and
a good reputation. These riches are lasting and priceless,
and this abundance is guaranteed by our obedience.

GOD'S PROMISE

If you give, you will receive. Your gift will return to you
in full measure, pressed down, shaken together to make
room for more, and running over.   *Luke 6:38*

CONTENTMENT

How does God's abundance satisfy the longings in my life?

GOD'S RESPONSE

If you only knew the gift God has for you and who I am, you would ask me, and I would give you living water. . . . People soon become thirsty again after drinking this water. But the water I give them takes away thirst altogether. It becomes a perpetual spring within them, giving them eternal life.　*John 4:10, 13-14*

Jesus replied, "I am the bread of life. No one who comes to me will ever be hungry again. Those who believe in me will never thirst."　*John 6:35*

I T'S A PRINCIPLE AS OLD AS CREATION that having more things does not bring great personal satisfaction. Only the Lord can fulfill your deepest longings because he built them into you from the moment he made you. When you learn how a relationship with him truly satisfies, you will stop longing for things that can never satisfy.

GOD'S PROMISE

He satisfies the thirsty and fills the hungry with good things.　*Psalm 107:9*

SCARCITY

What can I do in times of scarcity?

GOD'S RESPONSE

Does it mean he no longer loves us if we have trouble or calamity, or are persecuted, or are hungry or cold or in danger or threatened with death? . . . No, . . . overwhelming victory is ours through Christ, who loved us. *Romans 8:35-37*

Who else rescues the weak and helpless from the strong? Who else protects the poor and needy from those who want to rob them? *Psalm 35:10*

I am poor and needy, but the Lord is thinking about me right now. *Psalm 40:17*

IN TIMES OF SCARCITY, our greatest hope as believers is that this condition is temporary. God promises that for all eternity we will be free from trouble as we live with him in heaven. While it is difficult to accept that some people seem to get all the breaks on earth, God assures us that those who love and honor him will get all the breaks for eternity.

GOD'S PROMISE

Lord, where do I put my hope? My only hope is in you. *Psalm 39:7*

HOPE

How can I cultivate stronger hope?

GOD'S RESPONSE

Such things were written in the Scriptures long ago to teach us. They give us hope and encouragement as we wait patiently for God's promises.   *Romans 15:4*

Do not snatch your word of truth from me, for my only hope is in your laws. . . . May all who fear you find in me a cause for joy, for I have put my hope in your word. . . . I faint with longing for your salvation; but I have put my hope in your word. . . . You are my refuge and my shield; your word is my only source of hope. . . . I rise early, before the sun is up; I cry out for help and put my hope in your words.   *Psalm 119:43, 74, 81, 114, 147*

E VERY TIME YOU READ THE BIBLE, your hope for God's presence, comfort, rescue, and provision will be renewed and reinforced. God calls his Word "living" because he literally speaks to you through it. Cultivate stronger hope by reading and meditating on the promises of God's living Word.

GOD'S PROMISE

The word of God is full of living power.   *Hebrews 4:12*

HOPE

How can I keep hoping when God never seems to act?

GOD'S RESPONSE

Now that we are saved, we eagerly look forward to this freedom. For if you already have something, you don't need to hope for it.   *Romans 8:24*

What is faith? It is the confident assurance that what we hope for is going to happen. It is the evidence of things we cannot yet see.   *Hebrews 11:1*

When doubts filled my mind, your comfort gave me renewed hope and cheer.   *Psalm 94:19*

HOPE, BY DEFINITION, is expecting something that has not yet occurred. Faith and patience keep hope alive. Have faith that God will do what he has promised, and be patient while he does it in his time, in his way, and according to his plan. You can be absolutely certain that he is already acting on your behalf because God is trustworthy.

GOD'S CHALLENGE

Hope in the LORD; for with the LORD there is unfailing love and an overflowing supply of salvation.   *Psalm 130:7*

WAITING

How should I act during times of waiting?

GOD'S RESPONSE

The Kingdom of Heaven can be illustrated by the story of a man going on a trip. He called together his servants and gave them money to invest for him while he was gone. He gave five bags of gold to one. . . . After a long time their master returned from his trip and called them to give an account of how they had used his money. The servant to whom he had entrusted the five bags of gold said, "Sir, you gave me five bags of gold to invest, and I have doubled the amount." The master was full of praise. *Matthew 25:14-15, 19-21*

A S YOU WAIT, SERVE. As the servant in the parable was praised for his hard work and intelligence while the master was gone, you can be confident that Jesus wants you to faithfully and wisely serve him right where you are as you await your next instructions.

GOD'S PROMISE

Well done, my good and faithful servant. You have been faithful in handling this small amount, so now I will give you many more responsibilities. Let's celebrate together!   *Matthew 25:21*

FORGETTING

My life seems to be on hold right now. Has God forgotten me?

GOD'S RESPONSE

David was thirty years old when he began to reign, and he reigned forty years in all.   *2 Samuel 5:4*

Jesus was about thirty years old when he began his public ministry.   *Luke 3:23*

DAVID WAS ANOINTED as the next king of Israel when he was just a boy, but he didn't begin to reign until he was thirty. Much of that time was spent running from King Saul. Jesus also began his ministry when he was thirty. Paul spent years in prison. Though you might think God shouldn't have "wasted" their time, God knew better. David's waiting prepared him for the great work God called him to do. Paul's waiting gave him time to write several books of the New Testament. Your time "on hold" isn't wasted if you serve God where you are. Trust that his timing is better than your own.

GOD'S PROMISE

I cry out to God Most High, to God who will fulfill his purpose for me.   *Psalm 57:2*

How can I best use my time?

GOD'S RESPONSE

Teach us to make the most of our time, so that we may grow in wisdom.   *Psalm 90:12*

Be careful how you live, not as fools but as those who are wise. Make the most of every opportunity for doing good in these evil days. Don't act thoughtlessly, but try to understand what the Lord wants you to do. . . . Let the Holy Spirit fill and control you.   *Ephesians 5:15-18*

T IME IS A GIFT. In giving you time, God gives you the opportunity to serve him. Valuing time begins with seeing it from God's perspective. When you do, you learn that there is always time to accomplish God's plans for your life. When you give your time to the Lord, he promises that no opportunity will be wasted.

GOD'S CHALLENGE

How do you know what will happen tomorrow? For your life is like the morning fog—it's here a little while, then it's gone.   *James 4:14*

RESTLESSNESS

Sometimes I get restless. How can I rest in God?

GOD'S RESPONSE

Moses raised his hand and struck the rock twice with the staff.   *Numbers 20:11*

I felt obliged to offer the burnt offering myself before you came.   *1 Samuel 13:12*

The LORD placed you at my mercy back there in the cave, and some of my men told me to kill you, but I spared you. *1 Samuel 24:10*

R ESTLESSNESS CAN CAUSE YOU to act impatiently in ways you will later regret. Moses was restless about the Israelites' complaining and acted rashly by disobeying God. Saul also disobeyed God in his restlessness to go into battle. By contrast, though David had to wait a long time to become king after being anointed as a young man, he held out for God's timing, even when it seemed God had delivered Saul into his hands. When you feel restless in your time of waiting, thank God for where you are now and wait patiently to discover the reason as God's plan unfolds.

GOD'S PROMISE

Pray about everything. . . . If you do this, you will experience God's peace.   *Philippians 4:6-7*

CHANGE

How do I find the courage to face change?

GOD'S RESPONSE

LORD, you remain the same forever! Your throne continues from generation to generation.   *Lamentations 5:19*

I am the LORD, and I do not change.   *Malachi 3:6*

God above, who created all heaven's lights . . . never changes or casts shifting shadows.   *James 1:17*

S INCE CHANGE IN THIS LIFE IS INEVITABLE, take comfort in the Lord, the one who never changes. You can rely on his faithfulness, which has not changed from generation to generation; his love, which never shifts or dies; his promises, which are rock solid; and his salvation, which lasts for eternity. When your world spins out of control, cling to the one who controls the universe.

GOD'S PROMISE

God is not a man, that he should lie. He is not a human, that he should change his mind. Has he ever spoken and failed to act? Has he ever promised and not carried it through?   *Numbers 23:19*

CIRCUMSTANCES

Circumstances are difficult right now; is God controlling them?

GOD'S RESPONSE

The LORD does whatever pleases him throughout all heaven and earth.   *Psalm 135:6*

I am the one who creates the light and makes the darkness. I am the one who sends good times and bad times. I, the LORD, am the one who does these things.   *Isaiah 45:7*

GOD IS IN TOTAL CONTROL of your circumstances; he can change them at any time in any way. But he also makes it clear that we live in a sinful world in which he has allowed Satan to have a certain degree of control for a while. In the spiritual battle God sometimes allows evil to have the upper hand. But he also promises us a twofold victory. First, God loves to bring good out of bad circumstances if you remain on his side. Second, God promises ultimate and total victory over Satan and all evil when this world ends and God establishes his perfect Kingdom.

GOD'S PROMISE

We know that God causes everything to work together for the good of those who love God and are called according to his purpose for them.   *Romans 8:28*

SPIRITUAL EYESIGHT

How can I see God in the midst
of troubling circumstances?

GOD'S RESPONSE

When our enemies and the surrounding nations heard about it, they were frightened and humiliated. They realized that this work had been done with the help of our God. *Nehemiah 6:16*

Martha said to Jesus, "Lord, if you had been here, my brother would not have died. But even now I know that God will give you whatever you ask." *John 11:21-22*

When darkness overtakes the godly, light will come bursting in. *Psalm 112:4*

G OD CREATED YOU, LOVES YOU, and longs to have a relationship with you. He pursues you with persistent and unfailing love and draws you to himself. Today, ask God to open your spiritual eyes to see how events, conversations, "chance" meetings, thoughts, and open doors are God's hand reaching out to show you that he is nearby and at work in your life.

GOD'S PROMISE

God blesses those whose hearts are pure, for they will see God. *Matthew 5:8*

STABILITY

How should I respond to life's troubling circumstances?

GOD'S RESPONSE

Even though the fig trees have no blossoms, and there are no grapes on the vine; even though the olive crop fails, and the fields lie empty and barren; even though the flocks die in the fields, and the cattle barns are empty, yet I will rejoice in the LORD! I will be joyful in the God of my salvation. The Sovereign LORD is my strength! He will make me as surefooted as a deer and bring me safely over the mountains.   *Habakkuk 3:17-19*

A SPIRIT OF GRATITUDE AND PRAISE changes the way you look at life. Complaining connects you to your unhappiness. Gratitude and praise connect you to the source of real joy. When you make thanksgiving a regular part of your life, you stay focused on all God has done for you and continues to do for you. Expressing gratitude for God's help is a form of worship.

GOD'S CHALLENGE

Dear brothers and sisters, whenever trouble comes your way, let it be an opportunity for joy. For when your faith is tested, your endurance has a chance to grow. *James 1:2-3*

INTERCESSION

Sometimes I have no idea what to do next. What should I do?

GOD'S RESPONSE

The Holy Spirit helps us in our distress. For we don't even know what we should pray for, nor how we should pray. But the Holy Spirit prays for us with groanings that cannot be expressed in words. And the Father who knows all hearts knows what the Spirit is saying, for the Spirit pleads for us believers in harmony with God's own will. *Romans 8:26-27*

GOD WANTS TO HELP YOU make the right decisions. This is part of why he sent us the Holy Spirit—to be our voice of reason when we are lost and confused. The Bible says that even in times when we don't know what to ask or pray for, the Holy Spirit intercedes for us. When you are overwhelmed, confused, or uncertain, calm yourself in prayer. If you don't know what to say, the Spirit will pray on your behalf.

GOD'S PROMISE

The eyes of the LORD search the whole earth in order to strengthen those whose hearts are fully committed to him. *2 Chronicles 16:9*

DECISION-MAKING

Does God guide my decision-making?

GOD'S RESPONSE

Who are those who fear the LORD? He will show them the path they should choose.   *Psalm 25:12*

Learn to be wise, and develop good judgment. Don't forget or turn away from my words.   *Proverbs 4:5*

God is working in you, giving you the desire to obey him and the power to do what pleases him.   *Philippians 2:13*

PRAY FOR GOD TO GIVE you the desire to seek his guidance, and then to follow it. When you do, you will be able to make decisions that please him. God doesn't want to hide his will from you—he's not playing games with you. He wants to give you guidance; you just need to ask and then listen when he speaks.

GOD'S PROMISE

Seek his will in all you do, and he will direct your paths. *Proverbs 3:6*

CHOICES

How do I know if I'm making good or bad choices?

GOD'S RESPONSE

Oh, that you would choose life, that you and your descendants might live! Choose to love the LORD your God and to obey him and commit yourself to him, for he is your life. *Deuteronomy 30:19-20*

I have hidden your word in my heart, that I might not sin against you. *Psalm 119:11*

With many counselors, there is safety. *Proverbs 11:14*

THERE ARE THREE IMPORTANT WAYS to discern whether your decision is a good or bad one: (1) listen continually to God's voice in his Word to help you see what is right and what is wrong; (2) seek the counsel of God in prayer and the wise advice of reliable counselors; (3) avoid choices that benefit you at the expense of others. If you follow these guidelines, you will usually know with certainty the quality of your decisions.

GOD'S PROMISE

He guides me along right paths, bringing honor to his name. *Psalm 23:3*

DESIRES

How can I know if my desires match God's desires for me?

GOD'S RESPONSE

[David] sent someone to find out who she was, and he was told, "She is Bathsheba, the daughter of Eliam and the wife of Uriah the Hittite." Then David sent for her. *2 Samuel 11:3-4*

Fix your thoughts on what is true and honorable and right. Think about things that are pure and lovely and admirable. *Philippians 4:8*

DAVID'S SELFISH DESIRES overpowered his reason. His desire for Bathsheba caused him to commit adultery and to have her husband murdered, which resulted in much grief for his family. When wondering if what you desire is right or wrong, consider the long-term consequences. Is the object of your desire good, consistent with God's Word, and harmless to others? Answer that question, and you'll know which choice to make.

GOD'S CHALLENGE

Live a life of steady goodness so that only good deeds will pour forth. *James 3:13*

RESISTANCE

How can I resist the evil desires that are within me?

GOD'S RESPONSE

Don't let us yield to temptation, but deliver us from the evil one.   *Matthew 6:13*

The LORD made this covenant with you so that no man, woman, family, or tribe among you would turn away from the LORD our God to worship these gods of other nations.   *Deuteronomy 29:18*

Josiah removed all detestable idols.   *2 Chronicles 34:33*

THE MOST DANGEROUS TEMPTATIONS are often those which at first seem rather harmless. Sin often begins with just a small step away from God—then another and another, until you suddenly find yourself far from him. Rather than focusing on avoiding the ultimate temptation, avoid that first step that takes you slightly away from God. Commit yourself today to staying dead center on God's path.

GOD'S CHALLENGE

Let heaven fill your thoughts. Do not think only about things down here on earth. . . . So put to death the sinful, earthly things lurking within you.   *Colossians 3:2, 5*

CHANGE

How can God help me change the desires within my heart?

GOD'S RESPONSE

I will give you a new heart with new and right desires, and I will put a new spirit in you. I will take out your stony heart of sin and give you a new, obedient heart. *Ezekiel 36:26*

God stirred the hearts of the priests and Levites . . . to return to Jerusalem to rebuild the Temple of the Lord. *Ezra 1:5*

Now we can really serve God, not in the old way . . . but in the new way, by the Spirit. *Romans 7:6*

WHEN YOU COMMIT YOUR LIFE TO GOD, he gives you a new heart, a new nature, and a new desire to please him. When God stirs your heart, your desires will be in line with his will. Then it is your responsibility to act on those desires and serve him wholeheartedly.

GOD'S PROMISE

Those who become Christians become new persons. They are not the same anymore, for the old life is gone. A new life has begun! *2 Corinthians 5:17*

ENVY

How can I control my thoughts when I start to envy those around me?

GOD'S RESPONSE

This was their song: "Saul has killed his thousands, and David his ten thousands!" This made Saul very angry. *1 Samuel 18:7-8*

From that time on Saul kept a jealous eye on David. *1 Samuel 18:9*

Saul, who had a spear in his hand, suddenly hurled it at David.   *1 Samuel 18:10-11*

S AUL'S JEALOUSY BEGAN with envy, which festered until it tormented him. This torment led to uncontrolled rage, and finally to paranoia. Saul's jealousy consumed him until he could think of nothing else. Only murder would solve his problem. This story illustrates the power of envy to take over your life if you don't stop it. To defeat envy, you must stop comparing your situation with that of others and instead focus on what God has already given you.

GOD'S CHALLENGE

A relaxed attitude lengthens life; jealousy rots it away. *Proverbs 14:30*

EXPECTATIONS

What should I expect out of life?

GOD'S RESPONSE

I have told you all this so that you may have peace in me. Here on earth you will have many trials and sorrows. But take heart, because I have overcome the world.   *John 16:33*

Shouldn't we expect far greater glory when the Holy Spirit is giving life? . . . Since this new covenant gives us such confidence, we can be very bold.   *2 Corinthians 3:8, 12*

S OMETIMES, JESUS DOESN'T match our expectations—he talks about servanthood instead of getting ahead, of giving rather than getting, of sacrifice instead of luxury, of storing up treasure in heaven instead of on earth. When we stop expecting God to be what *we* want and start thinking of what *he* wants us to be, our expectations will begin to match his. Only then can we expect a truly fulfilling life. How do we know what God expects? It's all in the Bible. Read it and raise your expectations.

GOD'S PROMISE

We live with a wonderful expectation because Jesus Christ rose again from the dead. For God has reserved a priceless inheritance for his children. It is kept in heaven for you, pure and undefiled.   *1 Peter 1:3-4*

EXPECTATIONS

Are there expectations I shouldn't have?

GOD'S RESPONSE

They say to themselves, "Nothing bad will ever happen to us! We will be free of trouble forever!"   *Psalm 10:6*

When you dig a well, you may fall in. When you demolish an old wall, you could be bitten by a snake. When you work in a quarry, stones might fall and crush you! When you chop wood, there is danger with each stroke of your ax! Such are the risks of life.   *Ecclesiastes 10:8-9*

D ON'T EXPECT LIFE TO BE TROUBLE FREE just because you are a Christian. One misconception about Christianity is that life will be a bed of roses just because God is on your side. In fact, the Bible tells us that we might face trouble and oppression because of what we believe. You are in the middle of a spiritual battle—expect to get wounded. But also be assured of ultimate victory and eternal peace. What more can you expect than that?

GOD'S CHALLENGE

"My thoughts are completely different from yours," says the LORD. "And my ways are far beyond anything you could imagine."   *Isaiah 55:8*

DISCOURAGEMENT

I'm feeling a bit discouraged.
What can I do about that?

GOD'S RESPONSE

Why am I discouraged? Why so sad? I will put my hope in God! I will praise him again—my Savior and my God! Now I am deeply discouraged, but I will remember your kindness. *Psalm 42:5-6*

WITH EVERYTHING THAT CAN GO WRONG in life, it's no surprise that we often become discouraged. These verses tell us that the best antidote to discouragement is to remember God's mercy, praise him, sing a song to him in your heart, and become hopeful again. These things naturally lift you out of the dumps. God is your greatest encourager—let him build you up each day through his Word. This will lead you to encourage others, and some will return to you in gratitude, further encouraging you. When you are discouraged, you are particularly vulnerable to Satan's attacks, so stay close to your encouraging God. Encouragement is very effective in eliminating discouragement.

GOD'S PROMISE

God . . . encourages those who are discouraged.
2 Corinthians 7:6

DISCOURAGEMENT

How can I resist feelings of discouragement?

GOD'S RESPONSE

Don't be troubled. You trust God, now trust in me.
John 14:1

Don't get tired of doing what is good. Don't get discouraged and give up, for we will reap a harvest of blessing at the appropriate time.   *Galatians 6:9*

W HEN YOU FEEL DISCOURAGED, it is so easy to turn inward and become paralyzed with your own feelings and pain. It takes great effort when you are down, but refocus on God. Every day, he opens doors of opportunity that can bring purpose and meaning to you—helping someone in need, giving time to a good cause, writing a note of encouragement. When you lift your eyes from the ground, you will see the door that God has opened. Walk through it with courage; on the other side you will find great encouragement.

GOD'S PROMISE

This is what the LORD Almighty says: All this may seem impossible to you now, a small and discouraged remnant of God's people. But do you think this is impossible for me, the LORD Almighty?   *Zechariah 8:6*

SPIRITUAL DRYNESS

What can dampen my enthusiasm for Jesus and how can I guard against that?

GOD'S RESPONSE

The rocky soil represents those who hear the message and receive it with joy. But like young plants in such soil, their roots don't go very deep. At first they get along fine, but they wilt as soon as they have problems or are persecuted. *Matthew 13:20-21*

You must warn each other every day, as long as it is called "today," so that none of you will be deceived by sin and hardened against God. *Hebrews 3:13*

W HEN YOU GET SERIOUS about your faith, your enthusiasm for God grows by leaps and bounds. To prevent yourself from being shallow, read God's Word daily, study it, refuse to be deceived by sin, and learn how Satan tries to tempt you. Keep your focus on being a representative of Jesus Christ. God promises you more joy than you thought possible.

GOD'S PROMISE

When you obey me . . . you will be filled with my joy. Yes, your joy will overflow! *John 15:10-11*

DEPRESSION

I'm dealing with depression. Are these feelings sinful?

GOD'S RESPONSE

I am overwhelmed with trouble! Haven't I had enough pain already? And now the LORD has added more! I am weary of my own sighing and can find no rest.   *Jeremiah 45:3*

Come quickly, LORD, and answer me, for my depression deepens.   *Psalm 143:7*

YOUR FEELINGS OF DEPRESSION are not sinful. However, there's no denying that feelings have a lot of influence over your actions, which may become sinful if you are not careful. Jesus did not condemn those who were hurting or ill, and he will not condemn you for feeling depressed. Jesus' words are actually a tremendous encouragement because they acknowledge that undeserved suffering is part of human life, and that God can still be known and experienced in the midst of the darkest passages of life.

GOD'S PROMISE

I have told you all this so that you may have peace in me. Here on earth you will have many trials and sorrows. But take heart, because I have overcome the world.   *John 16:33*

DEFEAT

Is there ever a time to just give up?

GOD'S RESPONSE

Why is the LORD taking us to this country only to have us die in battle? Our wives and little ones will be carried off as slaves! Let's get out of here and return to Egypt! *Numbers 14:3*

SOMETIMES IT IS WISE TO QUIT, particularly when you are doing something wrong or you realize that your actions are futile or are hurting someone. But when God has called us to a task and we give up, we not only miss the great blessings of reaching our goal, but we might also incur discipline for not trusting God to help us get there. Just because God is in something doesn't make it easy. In fact, the harder the road, the stronger we become. If you know God is leading you and opening doors in a certain direction, don't give up just because the going gets tough. If anything, that should tell you that you are headed in the right direction. Keep moving forward boldly and with faith.

GOD'S PROMISE

Even though the olive crop fails, and the fields lie empty and barren . . . yet I will rejoice in the LORD! . . . He will make me as surefooted as a deer. *Habakkuk 3:17-19*

HOLINESS

What does it mean to be holy?

GOD'S RESPONSE

I plead with you to give your bodies to God. Let them be a living and holy sacrifice—the kind he will accept. *Romans 12:1*

TWO THINGS YOU SHOULD KNOW about holiness: (1) God doesn't expect you to be completely holy or perfect in this life, and (2) when you become a Christian, the Bible says you are set apart for a particular purpose. Remove yourself from sinful influences that distract you from the task God has given you. As you grow to be more like Jesus, your character will clearly show that something good and different is happening inside you. This will be attractive to many and they will want to know what it is. Holy living is not so much in what you avoid, but in how you relate to a holy God.

GOD'S PROMISE

Christ will make your hearts strong, blameless, and holy when you stand before God our Father on that day when our Lord Jesus comes with all those who belong to him. *1 Thessalonians 3:13*

VICTORY

What does it mean to live a "victorious" Christian life?

GOD'S RESPONSE

Every child of God defeats this evil world by trusting Christ to give the victory.   *1 John 5:4*

How we thank God, who gives us victory over sin and death through Jesus Christ our Lord!   *1 Corinthians 15:57*

I run straight to the goal with purpose in every step. *1 Corinthians 9:26*

S IN ALWAYS DESTROYS—sometimes dramatically and sometimes slowly. Sin harasses you, constantly drawing you away from your relationship with God. When temptation is allowed to lurk around the edges of your life, sin eventually finds a way into your heart. It is like a cancer that you fail to remove from your body. It is painful, it infects you, and it will eventually kill you. The more relentlessly you battle sin and remove it piece by piece from your life, the more you will experience the victorious Christian life and all the blessings that come with it. Achieving God's future rewards requires present obedience.

GOD'S PROMISE

The answer is in Jesus Christ our Lord.   *Romans 7:25*

CHANCE

Is God really in charge, or does everything happen by chance?

GOD'S RESPONSE

I am Joseph, your brother whom you sold into Egypt. But don't be angry with yourselves that you did this to me, for God did it. He sent me here ahead of you to preserve your lives. . . . It was God who sent me here, not you! *Genesis 45:4-5, 8*

F ROM OUR HUMAN PERSPECTIVE, the world and our individual lives often seem to be random and unpredictable, but God is ultimately in control. Joseph's story shows how God used even the seemingly unjust treatment of Joseph by his own brothers to fulfill God's plan. People's sinful ways do not ruin God's sovereign plans. In the end, you will discover that your life is like a tapestry; now you can only see sections of the back, with all its knots and loose ends. Some day you will see the front in its beautiful entirety—from God's perspective.

GOD'S PROMISE

You chart the path ahead of me and tell me where to stop and rest. Every moment you know where I am. *Psalm 139:3*

DYSFUNCTION

Can I overcome the challenges that come with growing up in a dysfunctional family?

GOD'S RESPONSE

It was by faith that Rahab the prostitute did not die with all the others in her city who refused to obey God. For she had given a friendly welcome to the spies.   *Hebrews 11:31*

Jephthah of Gilead was a great warrior. He was the son of Gilead, but his mother was a prostitute.   *Judges 11:1*

S OME OF THE HEROIC PEOPLE OF THE BIBLE overcame huge dysfunction when they put themselves into God's hands. Rahab the prostitute was spared because she saved the lives of two Israelite spies. Jephthah was a great warrior despite his upbringing. Don't use your family history as an excuse to continue dysfunctional or sinful behavior. Begin a new legacy. God wants to turn your disadvantages into advantages. With God's help, you can break the chain of sin handed down to you from long years of dysfunction.

GOD'S PROMISE

Because the Sovereign LORD helps me, I will not be dismayed. Therefore, I have set my face like a stone, determined to do his will. And I know that I will triumph.   *Isaiah 50:7*

GOSSIP

Why should we never listen to gossip?

GOD'S RESPONSE

A gossip goes around revealing secrets, but those who are trustworthy can keep a confidence.   *Proverbs 11:13*

Fire goes out for lack of fuel, and quarrels disappear when gossip stops.   *Proverbs 26:20*

GOSSIP BLENDS TWO OTHER SINS: lying and stealing. First, it uses half-truths or outright lies to throw doubt on the character of another person. Second, when you gossip about someone you are stealing something from them—an honorable reputation. You are also using information that belongs to them without their permission. Words that go out can't be gathered in again. With a single sentence you can ruin the reputation of another person. Gossip leads to divided communities, hatred, and premature judgment. Gossip has even been likened to murder because it is the assassination of someone's reputation and character.

GOD'S CHALLENGE

Let everything you say be good and helpful, so that your words will be an encouragement to those who hear them. *Ephesians 4:29*

CONFLICT

What are some ways to resolve a difficult conflict?

GOD'S RESPONSE

Isaac's men then dug another well, but again there was a fight over it. . . . He dug another well, and the local people finally left him alone.   *Genesis 26:21-22*

Barnabas . . . wanted to take along John Mark. But Paul disagreed strongly. . . . Their disagreement over this was so sharp that they separated.   *Acts 15:37-39*

The Lord's servants must not quarrel but must be kind to everyone. They must be . . . patient with difficult people. They should gently teach those who oppose the truth. *2 Timothy 2:24-25*

T O LIVE PEACEABLY WITH OTHERS does not mean avoiding conflict; instead, it means handling conflict appropriately. Conflict handled poorly leads to fractured relationships, and avoiding conflict altogether leads to unresolved hurt and anger. Rather, when conflict arises, rely on the Holy Spirit to keep you calm. Do not retaliate in anger, but respond with love. Do your best to restore harmony.

GOD'S CHALLENGE

Do your part to live in peace with everyone, as much as possible.   *Romans 12:18*

INNER CONFLICT

What is this conflict I seem to have within myself?

GOD'S RESPONSE

I don't understand myself at all, for I really want to do what is right, but I don't do it. Instead, I do the very thing I hate. . . . When I try not to do wrong, I do it anyway. . . . I love God's law . . . but there is another law at work within me that is at war with my mind. . . . Who will free me from this life that is dominated by sin? *Romans 7:15, 19, 22-24*

CHRISTIANS STRUGGLE DAILY with inner conflict. We have given our lives to Christ, but the old human nature still exists. We know the attitudes and behavior that Christ desires, but we also know how hard it is to live that way all the time. We wrestle with our desire to sin, to think more of ourselves than of others, to give in to temptation. There is a constant conflict going on within us. Ironically, good can come from this. It shows that our conscience is still sensitive to sin, and that we truly desire to do what is right. If there were no such struggle going on within you, it could indicate that you were too accepting of sin in your life.

GOD'S PROMISE

You will keep in perfect peace all who trust in you, whose thoughts are fixed on you!   *Isaiah 26:3*

PERSPECTIVE

How do we lose perspective?

GOD'S RESPONSE

The people of Israel said to Moses, "Look, we are doomed! We are dead! We are ruined! Everyone who even comes close to the Tabernacle of the LORD dies. Are we all doomed to die?"   *Numbers 17:12-13 (NLT2)*

THE PERSPECTIVE OF THE PEOPLE of Israel was completely opposite to reality. Instead of seeing the Tabernacle as a place to worship God, they saw it as a place to stay away from because of God. What had happened? Their perspective on God changed because their daily choices had changed from doing things for God to doing things for themselves. Obeying God is life's greatest accomplishment because it keeps us focused on what is really important and shows us that God supplies what we really need in great abundance. When we drift away from consistent obedience to God, we lose our eternal perspective.

GOD'S PROMISE

If you try to hang on to your life, you will lose it. But if you give up your life for my sake, you will save it. *Matthew 16:25 (NLT2)*

CRITICISM

How should I respond to criticism?

GOD'S RESPONSE

A wise person stays calm when insulted. An honest witness tells the truth; a false witness tells lies. Some people make cutting remarks, but the words of the wise bring healing. *Proverbs 12:16-18*

It is better to be criticized by a wise person than to be praised by a fool!   *Ecclesiastes 7:5*

My conscience is clear, but that isn't what matters. It is the Lord himself who will examine me and decide. *1 Corinthians 4:4*

I F YOU ARE CRITICIZED, remain calm and don't lash back. Evaluate whether the criticism is coming from a person with a reputation for wisdom and integrity. Ask yourself if the criticism is meant to heal or hurt. Is the criticism just and true? Maintain a clear conscience by being honest and trustworthy. This allows you to shrug off criticism that you know is unjustified. If criticism is justified, however, you are wise to listen and learn.

GOD'S PROMISE

If you listen to constructive criticism, you will be at home among the wise.   *Proverbs 15:31*

CRITICISM

What's the difference between judging others and constructive criticism?

GOD'S RESPONSE

Do not judge others, and you will not be judged. For you will be treated as you treat others. The standard you use in judging is the standard by which you will be judged. And why worry about a speck in your friend's eye when you have a log in your own?   *Matthew 7:1-3 (NLT2)*

ONE COACH BERATES A PLAYER PUBLICLY for making a mistake in a game. Another coach waits until the game is over and tells the player privately how to avoid making the same mistake again. Though no one likes criticism—even when it is constructive—we sometimes need it. But it is much easier to receive criticism when it is offered gently and in love, rather than in a harsh or humiliating way. A critic finds fault with no effort to see the person succeed or improve. One who offers constructive criticism invests in building a relationship and helping the other person become who God created him or her to be.

GOD'S CHALLENGE

You must make allowance for each other's faults and forgive the person who offends you. Remember, the Lord forgave you, so you must forgive others.   *Colossians 3:13*

COMPLIMENTS

What is the impact of complimenting and encouraging others?

GOD'S RESPONSE

Encourage each other and build each other up, just as you are already doing.   *1 Thessalonians 5:11*

Jonathan went to find David and encouraged him to stay strong in his faith in God.   *1 Samuel 23:16*

Hezekiah encouraged the Levites for the skill they displayed as they served the LORD.   *2 Chronicles 30:22*

E VERYONE NEEDS ENCOURAGEMENT. Think how you feel when someone sincerely expresses their confidence in you, builds you up, notices a job well done, or compliments your spiritual growth. Make others feel that way today. Speak well of them and to them. What you say could literally change their lives. Genuine compliments and encouragement make a huge difference in one's perspective on life.

GOD'S PROMISE

Worry weighs a person down; an encouraging word cheers a person up.   *Proverbs 12:25*

How do I show respect for others?

GOD'S RESPONSE

A despised Samaritan came along, and when he saw the man, he felt deep pity. Kneeling beside him, the Samaritan soothed his wounds.   *Luke 10:33-34*

Honor those who are your leaders in the Lord's work. *1 Thessalonians 5:12*

How can you claim that you have faith in our glorious Lord Jesus Christ if you favor some people more than others?   *James 2:1*

R ESPECT MEANS SHOWING MORE CONCERN for people than for agendas or social standing. God calls his people to respect and honor all other human beings, regardless of their race, status, social standing, or economic means. To show respect you should be fair, think highly of others, befriend them, encourage them, and treat them as equals. Remember that if you are a Christian, your mission is to show Jesus' reflection in you to others. How well have you been reflecting him?

GOD'S CHALLENGE

Love your Christian brothers and sisters.   *1 Peter 2:17*

ROUTINE

*As I settle into the activities of this season,
what should always be a part of my routine?*

GOD'S RESPONSE

You must commit yourselves wholeheartedly to these commands I am giving you today. Repeat them again and again to your children. Talk about them when you are at home and when you are away on a journey, when you are lying down and when you are getting up again. *Duteronomy 6:6-7*

[Daniel] prayed three times a day, just as he had always done, giving thanks to his God. *Daniel 6:10*

YOUR ROUTINE SHOULD ALWAYS include reading God's Word and sharing it with friends or family, praying, and attending church. Make these activities a priority, for you need them in order to have the peace, patience, and strength for everything else you do. Put God first and all other priorities will fall into order. Test God on this and watch him work powerfully in your life.

GOD'S PROMISE

I will bless you every day, and I will praise you forever. *Psalm 145:2*

CHURCH

Do I really need to go to church?

GOD'S RESPONSE

The church is his body; it is filled by Christ, who fills everything everywhere with his presence.   *Ephesians 1:23*

The human body has many parts, but the many parts make up only one body. So it is with the body of Christ. Some of us are Jews, some are Gentiles.   *1 Corinthians 12:12-13*

Let us not neglect our meeting together, as some people do, but encourage and warn each other.   *Hebrews 10:25*

ALL BELIEVERS TOGETHER FORM GOD'S FAMILY, and only by meeting together can we bond. The church exists in part to equip God's people to do God's work and to encourage them in their faith. The church is where Christians learn to work together in unity, reconciling differences among themselves in a way that is only possible in Christ by his Spirit. When we meet together, we can build each other up and help each other. The church needs you, because the body of Christ is not complete unless you are there.

GOD'S PROMISE

Upon this rock I will build my church, and all the powers of hell will not conquer it.   *Matthew 16:18*

CHURCH

Why is it important for me to be involved in the church?

GOD'S RESPONSE

You are citizens along with all of God's holy people. You are members of God's family. . . . We who believe are carefully joined together, becoming a holy temple for the Lord.   *Ephesians 2:19, 21*

Just as our bodies have many parts and each part has a special function, so it is with Christ's body. We are all parts of his one body, and each of us has different work to do. And since we are all one body in Christ . . . each of us [has] the ability to do certain things well.   *Romans 12:4-6*

G OD HAS GIVEN EACH OF US GIFTS—some of us are great organizers and administrators, whereas others are gifted musicians, teachers, or dishwashers. When everyone in the congregation uses their gifts to serve, the church becomes a powerful force for good, a strong witness for Jesus, and a mighty army to combat Satan's attacks against God's people in your community.

GOD'S PROMISE

What good fellowship we enjoyed as we walked together to the house of God.   *Psalm 55:14*

FELLOWSHIP

Why do I need the fellowship of other believers?

GOD'S RESPONSE

When he arrived and saw this proof of God's favor, he was filled with joy, and he encouraged the believers to stay true to the Lord.   *Acts 11:23*

Use his words to teach and counsel each other. Sing psalms and hymns and spiritual songs to God with thankful hearts.   *Colossians 3:16*

Since we are all one body in Christ, we belong to each other, and each of us needs all the others.   *Romans 12:5*

GOD CREATED YOU FOR RELATIONSHIPS. You truly cannot grow as a believer all by yourself—you need other Christians around you. Fellowship with other believers is necessary to keep you accountable, to correctly learn God's Word, to pray for each other's needs, to encourage one another, and to help you mature in faith.

GOD'S PROMISE

If we are living in the light of God's presence, just as Christ is, then we have fellowship with each other, and the blood of Jesus, his Son, cleanses us from every sin.
1 John 1:7

FELLOWSHIP

How is Christian fellowship different from other kinds of friendship?

GOD'S RESPONSE

I'm eager to encourage you in your faith, but I also want to be encouraged by yours. In this way, each of us will be a blessing to the other.   *Romans 1:12*

Confess your sins to each other and pray for each other so that you may be healed.   *James 5:16*

GOOD FRIENDS ARE A WONDERFUL GIFT, but fellowship among believers in Jesus (at church or in small groups) is unique because it invites the living God into your group. It brings together people who have a common perspective on life because they know their sins have been forgiven and that this impacts their freedom and their future. Christian fellowship provides a place for honest sharing about the things in life that really matter, encouragement to stay strong in the face of temptation and persecution, and unique supernatural help to deal with problems.

GOD'S PROMISE

Where two or three gather together because they are mine, I am there among them.   *Matthew 18:20*

CHARACTER

People say that Christians should have "good character." What does that mean?

GOD'S RESPONSE

You are a holy people, who belong to the LORD your God. Of all the people on earth, the LORD your God has chosen you to be his own special treasure.   *Deuteronomy 7:6*

God created people in his own image.   *Genesis 1:27*

GOD MADE US IN HIS OWN IMAGE. We are to reflect his nature, including his character traits. We have the potential to be loving, truthful, patient, forgiving, kind, and faithful. Being made in God's image does not mean you are a god, or even godly, but that you have many of the characteristics of God himself. God wants us to use them as he uses them—to honor and benefit others.

GOD'S PROMISE

Those who are wise will shine as bright as the sky, and those who turn many to righteousness will shine like stars forever.   *Daniel 12:3*

CHARACTER

Why does character matter?

GOD'S RESPONSE

My child, never forget the things I have taught you. Store my commands in your heart, for they will give you a long and satisfying life. Never let loyalty and kindness get away from you! Wear them like a necklace; write them deep within your heart. Then you will find favor with both God and people, and you will gain a good reputation. *Proverbs 3:1-4*

Y OU CAN FOOL PEOPLE FOR A WHILE by your words and actions, but who you are on the inside will ultimately show itself on the outside. Your words and actions will reflect your heart. Character is so important because it is a direct reflection of your heart. For example, committing to worship shows that God comes first in your heart. Committing yourself to kindness shows a commitment to serving others. What is your heart committed to? If you aren't sure, then others probably aren't either.

GOD'S CHALLENGE

Even children are known by the way they act, whether their conduct is pure and right.   *Proverbs 20:11*

REFLECTION

How is character developed?

GOD'S RESPONSE

Remember how the LORD your God led you through the wilderness for forty years, humbling you and testing you to prove your character, and to find out whether or not you would really obey his commands.   *Deuteronomy 8:2*

Obedience is far better than sacrifice. Listening to him is much better than offering the fat of rams.   *1 Samuel 15:22*

YOU ARE NOT BORN WITH GODLY CHARACTER; it is a process that comes only through time, experience, humility, and testing. When you realize you are not all you'd like to be, when you make a commitment to know God and read his Word, and when you face tough challenges and choose wisely, your character will increasingly become a better reflection of God's character.

GOD'S PROMISE

Endurance develops strength of character in us, and character strengthens our confident expectation of salvation.   *Romans 5:4*

PRODUCTIVITY

What does the Bible mean when it says my life should produce "fruit"?

GOD'S RESPONSE

When the Holy Spirit controls our lives, he will produce this kind of fruit in us: love, joy, peace, patience, kindness, goodness, faithfulness, gentleness, and self-control. *Galatians 5:22-23*

A good person produces good deeds from a good heart. *Luke 6:45*

THE "FRUIT" THE BIBLE TALKS ABOUT is the "fruit of the Spirit," character qualities that the Holy Spirit wants you to allow him to develop in your life. But he will not force you to have these qualities. When you accept Jesus as Savior, the Holy Spirit literally comes to live in you. Only he has the power to put your old nature to death, giving you a new nature that produces good fruit, or good character traits. Your life will continue to bear good fruit only as you stay connected to the source of growth.

GOD'S CHALLENGE

I am the vine; you are the branches. Those who remain in me, and I in them, will produce much fruit. For apart from me you can do nothing.   *John 15:5*

LOVE

What is love?

GOD'S RESPONSE

Love is patient and kind. Love is not jealous or boastful or proud or rude. Love does not demand its own way. Love is not irritable, and it keeps no record of when it has been wronged. It is never glad about injustice but rejoices whenever the truth wins out. Love never gives up, never loses faith, is always hopeful, and endures through every circumstance.   *1 Corinthians 13:4-7*

A HEALTHY DEFINITION OF LOVE is crucial to understanding the central message of the Bible. According to the Bible, love is not about sexuality, nor is it primarily a feeling. Love is a commitment, a consistent and determined decision to think of others first, to put their needs above your own, and to serve them. God loves us in that way, and he gives us the ability to love others.

GOD'S PROMISE

There are three things that will endure—faith, hope, and love—and the greatest of these is love.
1 Corinthians 13:13

CHILDLIKENESS

How can I do a better job of accepting God's love?

GOD'S RESPONSE

Let the children come to me. Don't stop them! For the Kingdom of God belongs to such as these.   *Luke 18:16*

Jesus prayed this prayer: "O Father, Lord of heaven and earth, thank you for hiding the truth from those who think themselves so wise and clever, and for revealing it to the childlike."   *Matthew 11:25*

The LORD protects those of childlike faith; I was facing death, and then he saved me.   *Psalm 116:6*

YOU BEGIN TO ACCEPT GOD'S LOVE as you increase in humility and decrease in self-sufficiency. Jesus encourages you to receive his love with the same kind of trust a little child shows. A little child just loves to be loved and simply soaks it up without needing to know why he or she is loved. Receiving God's love is an act of simple faith. You have to be humble enough to know you need God and can't make it through life or eternity without him.

GOD'S PROMISE

I will be faithful to you and make you mine, and you will finally know me as LORD.   *Hosea 2:20*

LOVE

How can I be more loving toward others?

GOD'S RESPONSE

If anyone says, "I am living in the light," but hates a Christian brother or sister, that person is still living in darkness.   *1 John 2:9*

If we love each other, God lives in us, and his love has been brought to full expression through us.   *1 John 4:12*

We love each other as a result of his loving us first.   *1 John 4:19*

IF YOU ARE A CHRISTIAN, rejecting another Christian is not an option. When you find a fellow believer to be unlovable, stop to think how unlovable you can be at times. When you consider that God loves you anyway, you may find it in your heart to be more accepting of others. The only reason we can love others, and they can love us, is because God loved us first—to the point of dying for us. Remembering his great love for you should soften your heart and allow you to love others, even when they don't seem lovable.

GOD'S PROMISE

Your love for one another will prove to the world that you are my disciples.   *John 13:35*

ENEMIES

What does it mean to love my enemies?

GOD'S RESPONSE

All of you should be of one mind, full of sympathy toward each other, loving one another with tender hearts and humble minds. Don't repay evil for evil. Don't retaliate when people say unkind things about you. Instead, pay them back with a blessing. That is what God wants you to do, and he will bless you for it.   *1 Peter 3:8-9*

S HOWING LOVE TO ONE'S ENEMIES is always unreasonable—until you realize that you were an enemy of God before he forgave you. When you love an enemy, you see him or her as Christ does, as a person in need of grace. Getting to that point takes prayer. You can't pray for someone without feeling compassion for them. This is how you can refrain from retaliating when they hurt you, and this is how God can turn an enemy into a friend.

GOD'S CHALLENGE

If your enemies are hungry, feed them. If they are thirsty, give them something to drink. . . . Don't let evil get the best of you, but conquer evil by doing good.
Romans 12:20-21

JOY

What is joy?

GOD'S RESPONSE

Let the godly rejoice. Let them be glad in God's presence. Let them be filled with joy.   *Psalm 68:3*

Our hearts ache, but we always have joy. We are poor, but we give spiritual riches to others. We own nothing, and yet we have everything.   *2 Corinthians 6:10*

JOY IS THE CELEBRATION OF WALKING in God's presence. It is an inner happiness that lasts despite the circumstances around you because it is based on a relationship with Jesus Christ. If you are a believer, this gives you absolute confidence that God is personal and involved in your life, that evil will one day be defeated forever, and that heaven is a reality. With this new perspective, you realize that your feelings may go up and down, but joy runs so deep that nothing can take it away.

GOD'S PROMISE

Those who have been ransomed by the LORD will return to Jerusalem, singing songs of everlasting joy. Sorrow and mourning will disappear, and they will be overcome with joy and gladness.   *Isaiah 51:11*

Where does joy come from?

GOD'S RESPONSE

May all who search for you be filled with joy and gladness. May those who love your salvation repeatedly shout, "The Lord is great!"   *Psalm 40:16*

Consider the joy of those corrected by God! Do not despise the chastening of the Almighty when you sin. *Job 5:17*

I know the Lord is always with me. . . . No wonder my heart is filled with joy.   *Psalm 16:8-9*

THE LORD HIMSELF IS THE SOURCE of true joy. The more you love him, know him, walk with him, and become like him, the greater your joy will be. Even times of discipline can be considered joyful because you know that God loves you enough to correct you.

GOD'S PROMISE

The joy of the Lord is your strength!   *Nehemiah 8:10*

JOYFULNESS

How can I be more joyful?

GOD'S RESPONSE

Always be full of joy in the Lord. I say it again—rejoice!
Philippians 4:4

I am overcome with joy because of your unfailing love,
for you have seen my troubles, and you care about the
anguish of my soul.   *Psalm 31:7*

Always be joyful.   *1 Thessalonians 5:16*

THERE ARE AREAS OF THE CHRISTIAN LIFE that are
very serious—confronting sin and its consequences,
church discipline, fighting evil. But there is also great
delight in knowing that the God of the universe loves
you, has a plan for you, and made this wonderful world
for you. In fact, he tells you to serve him enthusiastically.
The Bible urges you to serve God with all of your being—
with an enthusiasm that comes from deep within your
heart and soul. Joy and enthusiasm light the fire of service.

GOD'S PROMISE

You love him even though you have never seen him.
Though you do not see him, you trust him; and even
now you are happy with a glorious, inexpressible joy.
1 Peter 1:8

POTENTIAL

What does God think when he looks at me with all my faults and limitations?

GOD'S RESPONSE

Gideon . . . had been threshing wheat at the bottom of a winepress to hide the grain from the Midianites. The angel of the LORD appeared to him and said, "Mighty hero, the LORD is with you! . . . Go with the strength you have and rescue Israel from the Midianites." . . .

"But Lord," Gideon replied, "how can I rescue Israel? . . . I am the least in my entire family!"   *Judges 6:11-12, 14-15*

THE ANGEL OF THE LORD GREETED Gideon by calling him a "mighty hero." Was he talking to the right person? This was a man hiding in a winepress from his enemies, a man who claimed he was "the least" of his family. But God calls out the best in us, and he sees more in us than we see in ourselves. We look at our limitations, but God looks at our potential. If you want to change your outlook, learn to see life from God's perspective. He sees you for what he intended you to be as well as for what you are.

GOD'S PROMISE

God, who began the good work within you, will continue his work until it is finally finished on that day when Christ Jesus comes back again.   *Philippians 1:6*

BACKSLIDING

Why do we forget to stay close to God?

GOD'S RESPONSE

Beware that in your plenty you do not forget the LORD your God and disobey his commands. . . . For when you have become full and prosperous and have built fine homes to live in . . . be careful. Do not become proud at that time and forget the LORD your God.   *Deuteronomy 8:11-12, 14*

I T IS EASY TO FEEL DISAPPOINTMENT after fulfilling a major commitment. We are the most vulnerable after a victory, when pride can make us feel overconfident. There is no longer a big goal before us and our emotions can take a nosedive. In no time, we can go from elation to discouragement. Here are several ways to stay close to God: (1) declare your allegiance to him out loud every day; (2) make the choice daily to live the way God wants you to; (3) obey God's Word faithfully and deliberately; (4) find a place to serve God again right away, and do so with energy and enthusiasm. With God on your mind each day, it is hard to forget him.

GOD'S PROMISE

You will live in joy and peace. The mountains and hills will burst into song, and the trees of the field will clap their hands!   *Isaiah 55:12*

Is there any hope for world peace?

GOD'S RESPONSE

God blesses those who work for peace, for they will be called the children of God.   *Matthew 5:9*

A child is born to us, a son is given to us. . . . These will be his royal titles . . . Prince of Peace.   *Isaiah 9:6*

He will remove all of their sorrows, and there will be no more death or sorrow or crying or pain. For the old world and its evils are gone forever.   *Revelation 21:4*

W AR IS AN INEVITABLE CONSEQUENCE of human sin. Christians are called upon to pray and work for peace in the world. Just think how much worse it would be if we stopped working and praying for peace. But ultimately, because of mankind's sinful nature, war will not end until Jesus, the Prince of Peace, returns, and then there will finally be peace forever. But that doesn't excuse you from doing your part every day to promote peace now.

GOD'S PROMISE

The LORD will settle international disputes. All the nations will beat their swords into plowshares and their spears into pruning hooks. All wars will stop, and military training will come to an end.   *Micah 4:3*

PEACE WITH GOD

How can I find peace with God?

GOD'S RESPONSE

He was wounded and crushed for our sins. He was beaten that we might have peace. He was whipped, and we were healed!   *Isaiah 53:5*

There will be glory and honor and peace from God for all who do good.   *Romans 2:10*

Those who love your law have great peace and do not stumble.   *Psalm 119:165*

TO BE AT PEACE WITH GOD, you have to stop fighting him for control of your life and stop resisting his plan for you. After all, he created you, he knows you better than you know yourself, and he knows what is best for you. You will find peace with God when you give up your pride and accept his redemption, not only for your soul, but for your life on earth as well.

GOD'S PROMISE

Since we have been made right in God's sight by faith, we have peace with God because of what Jesus Christ our Lord has done for us.   *Romans 5:1*

How can I make peace with others?

GOD'S RESPONSE

Live in harmony and peace. Then the God of love and peace will be with you.   *2 Corinthians 13:11*

Never pay back evil for evil to anyone. . . . Do your part to live in peace with everyone.   *Romans 12:17-18*

TOO OFTEN WE REACT TO DIFFERENCES of opinion with the swords we know as our tongues. Angry debates, insults, accusations, verbal manipulation, and character assassination are some of the ways we try to make ourselves and our agenda the "winner." But the victory isn't worth it. Too many people are wounded, too many relationships are hurt. Constructive disagreements are essential to deep relationships, but conflict that divides the church breaks God's heart. This misdirects energy that should be spent on discipleship, evangelism, worship, and missions. It also sabotages our witness to the world (John 17:20-23). Express your opinions in a way that honors and serves those who differ from you (Proverbs 12:18).

GOD'S CHALLENGE

Work hard at living in peace with others.   *Psalm 34:14*

PATIENCE

How can I develop more patience?

GOD'S RESPONSE

May God, who gives this patience and encouragement, help you live in complete harmony with each other—each with the attitude of Christ Jesus toward the other.   *Romans 15:5*

We also pray that you will be strengthened with his glorious power so that you will have all the patience and endurance you need.   *Colossians 1:11*

PATIENCE AND PERSPECTIVE GO HAND IN HAND. When you are always focused on your own agenda and priorities, you will find yourself impatient much of the time because life rarely goes the way you want it to. If you take the larger perspective that life is a journey and not a straight line between two points, you will realize that what you do along the way is more important than getting there. This allows you to wait patiently and learn when things don't go your way, and to find ways to serve others on the detours of daily life.

GOD'S CHALLENGE

Be glad for all God is planning for you. Be patient in trouble, and always be prayerful.   *Romans 12:12*

IMPATIENCE

What are some of the consequences of impatience?

GOD'S RESPONSE

Samuel said, "What is this you have done?"

Saul replied, "I saw my men scattering from me, and you didn't arrive when you said you would, and the Philistines are at Micmash ready for battle. So I said, 'The Philistines are ready to march against us, and I haven't even asked for the LORD's help!' So I felt obliged to offer the burnt offering myself before you came."

"How foolish!" Samuel exclaimed. "You have disobeyed the command of the LORD your God."   *1 Samuel 13:11-13*

G OD USES LIFE CIRCUMSTANCES TO develop your patience. Patient waiting is harder than running ahead, but it may keep you from running into disaster. Saul's impatience led him to sin and caused him to lose his kingdom. Learning to wait is difficult, but the only way to learn patience is to practice it—by waiting!

GOD'S PROMISE

Don't be impatient for the LORD to act! Travel steadily along his path. He will honor you, giving you the land. *Psalm 37:34*

WAITING

What does it mean to "wait on the Lord"?

GOD'S RESPONSE

I wait quietly before God, for my salvation comes from him. . . . I wait quietly before God, for my hope is in him. *Psalm 62:1, 5*

I waited patiently for the LORD to help me, and he turned to me and heard my cry.   *Psalm 40:1*

THE ABILITY TO WAIT QUIETLY for something is evidence of strong character. Waiting on the Lord is the patient confidence that what he promises for our life now and in the future will come true. When we are able to wait quietly for God to act without getting restless and agitated, we show we trust his timing fully. What a confident and peaceful way to live!

GOD'S PROMISE

Those who wait on the LORD will find new strength. They will fly high on wings like eagles. They will run and not grow weary. They will walk and not faint. *Isaiah 40:31*

KINDNESS

Is kindness overrated? Why should I be kind to others?

GOD'S RESPONSE

Be kind to each other, tenderhearted, forgiving one another, just as God through Christ has forgiven you.
Ephesians 4:32

When you are harvesting your crops and forget to bring in a bundle of grain from your field, don't go back to get it. Leave it for the foreigners, orphans, and widows. Then the LORD your God will bless you in all you do.   *Deuteronomy 24:19*

Kindness is an act of love, and after loving God, loving others is the next greatest command. A simple but profound truth is that God blesses you for acts of kindness in ways that are best for you. You may think that having more money would be a great blessing, but God may know that a close friendship, a deeper relationship with him, or victory over a bad habit may be more valuable. As our kindness toward others blesses them, we in turn will be blessed by God's kindness.

GOD'S CHALLENGE

Never let loyalty and kindness get away from you! Wear them like a necklace; write them deep within your heart.
Proverbs 3:3

KINDNESS

How can I show kindness to others?

GOD'S RESPONSE

The way you live will always honor and please the Lord, and you will continually do good, kind things for others. All the while, you will learn to know God better and better. *Colossians 1:10*

I myself have gained much joy and comfort from your love, my brother, because your kindness has so often refreshed the hearts of God's people. *Philemon 1:7*

K INDNESS IS NOT A SINGLE ACT but a lifestyle. It is the habit of being helpful, encouraging, sympathetic, and giving—what you do for others that says, "I'm thinking of you." Even in confrontation you can be kind. You practice kindness in all you do and say, always treating others as you would want to be treated. When you do that, you bring great refreshment to everyone you meet and you honor and please the Lord. Your kindness today may pass on to many generations and leave a lasting impression on more people than you realize.

GOD'S PROMISE

Your own soul is nourished when you are kind.
Proverbs 11:17

KINDNESS

How does God show his kindness?

GOD'S RESPONSE

God our Savior showed us his kindness and love. He saved us, not because of the good things we did, but because of his mercy. He washed away our sins and gave us a new life through the Holy Spirit. He generously poured out the Spirit upon us because of what Jesus Christ our Savior did. He declared us not guilty because of his great kindness. And now we know that we will inherit eternal life. These things I have told you are all true. I want you to insist on them so that everyone who trusts in God will be careful to do good deeds all the time.   *Titus 3:4-8*

BY GOD'S KINDNESS YOU WERE GIVEN the free gift of salvation even though you didn't deserve it. Because of God's kindness, you have forgiveness and freedom from guilt. Because of God's kindness, you have been blessed beyond your wildest dreams because you have secured a perfect life for all eternity in heaven.

GOD'S PROMISE

If they are saved by God's kindness, then it is not by their good works. For in that case, God's wonderful kindness would not be what it really is—free and undeserved.
Romans 11:6

GOODNESS

How should I "be good"?

GOD'S RESPONSE

She must be well respected by everyone because of the good she has done. . . . Has she been kind to strangers? . . . Has she helped those who are in trouble?   *1 Timothy 5:10*

The Kingdom of God is not a matter of what we eat or drink, but of living a life of goodness and peace and joy in the Holy Spirit.   *Romans 14:17*

G OODNESS IS NOT MERELY BEING TALENTED at something, as in "he is good at golfing." Goodness is a composite of many qualities such as being kind, helpful, loving, pleasant, generous, and gentle. These qualities exhibit our likeness to God. When Christ takes control of your heart, you will begin doing good deeds, which if practiced over a lifetime, will be defined as goodness.

GOD'S PROMISE

You are a chosen people. You are a kingdom of priests, God's holy nation, his very own possession. This is so you can show others the goodness of God, for he called you out of the darkness into his wonderful light. *1 Peter 2:9*

GOODNESS

In what ways can I see God's goodness?

GOD'S RESPONSE

In the beginning God created the heavens and the earth. . . . And God saw that it was good. *Genesis 1:1, 4*

Surely your goodness and unfailing love will pursue me all the days of my life, and I will live in the house of the LORD forever. *Psalm 23:6*

The LORD replied, "I will make all my goodness pass before you, and I will call out my name, 'the LORD,' to you. I will show kindness to anyone I choose, and I will show mercy to anyone I choose." *Exodus 33:19*

G OD'S GOODNESS CAN BE SEEN in creation. God could have created a black-and-white world with no scents or sounds or tastes, but out of his goodness came incredible beauty and variety. His goodness is also revealed in his kindness and unfailing love in offering you the gift of salvation and eternal life, not to mention family, friends, and too many other gifts to count.

GOD'S PROMISE

The LORD is wonderfully good to those who wait for him and seek him. *Lamentations 3:25*

GRATITUDE

How can I show my appreciation to God?

GOD'S RESPONSE

I will tell everyone of your justice and goodness, and I will praise you all day long.   *Psalm 35:28*

He fell face down on the ground at Jesus' feet, thanking him for what he had done.   *Luke 17:16*

Devote yourselves to prayer with an alert mind and a thankful heart.   *Colossians 4:2*

I will offer you a sacrifice of thanksgiving.   *Psalm 116:17*

W E PRAY OFTEN WHEN WE HAVE A NEED. We pray often when we want something from God. But what happens when God answers prayer? Do we remember to pray as often and as fervently in thanking him for answered prayer? Check up on yourself to see how thankful you are for answered prayer.

GOD'S PROMISE

Praise the Lord! Give thanks to the Lord, for he is good! His faithful love endures forever.   *Psalm 106:1*

FAITHFULNESS

What are the benefits of faithfulness?

GOD'S RESPONSE

If we are faithful to the end . . . we will share in all that belongs to Christ.   *Hebrews 3:14*

You have been faithful with the little I entrusted to you, so you will be governor of ten cities as your reward. *Luke 19:17*

My servant Caleb is different from the others. He has remained loyal to me, and I will bring him into the land he explored. His descendants will receive their full share of that land.   *Numbers 14:24*

FAITHFULNESS BRINGS REWARDS—both in this life and for eternity. God is aware of the way you approach life and is pleased when you are loyal to him. Others also recognize a person with the reputation for faithfulness and loyalty. An individual avoids trouble and gains security from this lifestyle. The best reason to be faithful, however, is that God is faithful to you.

GOD'S PROMISE

Remain faithful even when facing death, and I will give you the crown of life.   *Revelation 2:10*

FAITHFULNESS

How do I develop faithfulness?

GOD'S RESPONSE

Be faithful to the LORD your God as you have done until now. For the LORD has driven out great and powerful nations for you, and no one has yet been able to defeat you. Each one of you will put to flight a thousand of the enemy, for the LORD your God fights for you, just as he has promised. *Joshua 23:8-10*

No accounting was required from the construction supervisors, because they were honest and faithful workers. *2 Kings 12:15*

FAITHFULNESS INVOLVES loyalty, honesty, and commitment. Those who understand this are respected and trusted. You develop faithfulness by starting with the small tasks in life and working up to greater causes. Vow to be honest, committed, and faithful to the people in your life and to the work God has given you to do. Some day, when God greets you at heaven's door, he will say to you, "Well done, good and faithful servant."

GOD'S PROMISE

He guards the paths of justice and protects those who are faithful to him. *Proverbs 2:8*

FAITHFULNESS

How is God faithful?

GOD'S RESPONSE

He is the Rock; his work is perfect. Everything he does is just and fair. He is a faithful God who does no wrong; how just and upright he is!   *Deuteronomy 32:4*

God . . . always does just what he says, and he is the one who invited you into this wonderful friendship with his Son, Jesus Christ our Lord.   *1 Corinthians 1:9*

Your unfailing love is higher than the heavens. Your faithfulness reaches to the clouds.   *Psalm 108:4*

GOD ALWAYS DOES WHAT HE SAYS HE WILL DO. As you read the Bible, you will discover many promises from God that have already been fulfilled. That means that when you read the promises yet to come, you can count on God's faithfulness to fulfill them. God is faithful to you because he promises that his love for you will never end. How faithful are you to God?

GOD'S PROMISE

Give thanks to the LORD, for he is good! His faithful love endures forever.   *1 Chronicles 16:34*

GENTLENESS

What does gentleness accomplish? Won't everyone just walk all over me if I am gentle?

GOD'S RESPONSE

When the Holy Spirit controls our lives, he will produce this kind of fruit in us: love, joy, peace, patience, kindness, goodness, faithfulness, gentleness, and self-control. Here there is no conflict with the law.   *Galatians 5:22-23*

You should be known for the beauty that comes from within, the unfading beauty of a gentle and quiet spirit, which is so precious to God.   *1 Peter 3:4*

L OVE IS GENTLE, NOT ROUGH. God is love. Mercy is gentle, not cruel. God is merciful. Gentleness does not mean that you let others take advantage of you. God is the perfect example of gentleness, and yet he is also a mighty warrior able to defeat the powers of hell. In God's eyes, gentle people are the most powerful and influential in the world because they make an impact without conflict or war. Gentleness may be the most powerful weapon in your arsenal. You will accomplish more with gentleness than with coercion.

GOD'S PROMISE

God blesses those who are gentle and lowly, for the whole earth will belong to them.   *Matthew 5:5*

GENTLENESS

How is God gentle?

GOD'S RESPONSE

Correct me, LORD, but please be gentle. Do not correct me in anger, for I would die.   *Jeremiah 10:24*

The LORD is like a father to his children, tender and compassionate to those who fear him. For he understands how weak we are; he knows we are only dust. *Psalm 103:13-14*

GOD DOES NOT ALWAYS OPERATE in the realm of the spectacular. In fact, the spectacular does not always get our attention. Jesus' gentle words often made a greater impact upon people than his dramatic miracles. Sometimes your quiet and gentle words are just what are needed as an encouragement and challenge to a friend. It is not always the loudest voice that is heard. The next time you need to get a message across to someone, a gentle response in the midst of an uproar may be just what a person needs to hear.

GOD'S PROMISE

You have given me the shield of your salvation. Your right hand supports me; your gentleness has made me great.   *Psalm 18:35*

DISRESPECT

In what ways do people show disrespect to God?

GOD'S RESPONSE

Do not misuse the name of the LORD your God.
Exodus 20:7

Do not treat my holy name as common and ordinary.
Leviticus 22:32

TOO OFTEN WE TREAT GOD AS ORDINARY, forgetting that he is completely holy. We must be extremely careful to treat God with the reverence he deserves. Thinking of him as "Santa Claus" or "The Old Man Upstairs" is disrespectful, as is using his name to swear or spice up your language. Treating God as ordinary shows that you do not understand who God is or what he can do. Respect for God means that you show reverence for his name. Anyone who can design and build a magnificent cathedral would be respected. Even more, we should respect the one who designed and created the universe.

GOD'S PROMISE

The LORD watches over those who fear him.
Psalm 33:18

TEMPTATION

Why do I give in to temptation?

GOD'S RESPONSE

Anyone who even looks at a woman with lust in his eye has already committed adultery with her in his heart. *Matthew 5:28*

Late one afternoon David . . . went for a stroll on the roof of the palace. As he looked out over the city, he noticed a woman of unusual beauty taking a bath. He sent someone to find out who she was. *2 Samuel 11:2-3*

TEMPTATION OFTEN BEGINS with the eyes and travels quickly to the heart. What you do immediately after you notice something tempting will affect your thoughts and actions for a long time. If you let your eyes linger where they shouldn't be looking, your mind will start finding ways to justify your gaze, and your heart will start tugging you in that direction. The first step in avoiding temptation is to take your eyes off that which is tempting.

GOD'S CHALLENGE

I discovered that a seductive woman is more bitter than death. Her passion is a trap, and her soft hands will bind you. Those who please God will escape from her, but sinners will be caught in her snare. *Ecclesiastes 7:26*

SELF-CONTROL

What is self-control? Why is it necessary?

GOD'S RESPONSE

When the Holy Spirit controls our lives, he will produce this kind of fruit in us: love, joy, peace . . . and self-control.   *Galatians 5:22-23*

Spend your time and energy in training yourself for spiritual fitness. Physical exercise has some value, but spiritual exercise is much more important, for it promises a reward in both this life and the next.   *1 Timothy 4:7-8*

SELF-CONTROL IS ONE of the hardest character traits to achieve because it means denying what comes naturally to your sinful nature and replacing that with a controlled, godly response. Self-control is a lifelong struggle because just when you think you have an area of your life mastered, another area gets out of control. Some of the hardest things to control are our thoughts, our words, and our physical appetites. It is only with the help of the Holy Spirit that we achieve self-control. But when we do, we please God and please others.

GOD'S CHALLENGE

It is better to have self-control than to conquer a city.
Proverbs 16:32

SELF-CONTROL

What are some steps to learning self-control?

GOD'S RESPONSE

Keep me from deliberate sins! Don't let them control me. Then I will be free of guilt and innocent of great sin. *Psalm 19:13*

God wants you to be holy, so you should keep clear of all sexual sin. Then each of you will control your body and live in holiness and honor—not in lustful passion. *1 Thessalonians 4:3-5*

GOD WANTS US TO EXERCISE SELF-CONTROL over what we think, what we say, and what we do. He wants us to live as followers of God—not as mindless followers of the godless ways of culture. We can do this by honestly assessing our weaknesses; determining that they will no longer rule us; appealing to the Holy Spirit to help us stand strong against temptation; confessing to God with humility when we mess up; and giving glory to God when we are victorious.

GOD'S CHALLENGE

All athletes practice strict self-control. They do it to win a prize that will fade away, but we do it for an eternal prize. *1 Corinthians 9:25*

WORDS

How can I exercise control over my words?

GOD'S RESPONSE

Take control of what I say, O LORD, and keep my lips sealed.   *Psalm 141:3*

I tell you this, that you must give an account on judgment day of every idle word you speak.   *Matthew 12:36*

If you claim to be religious but don't control your tongue, you are just fooling yourself, and your religion is worthless. *James 1:26*

EXERCISING SELF-CONTROL over your words involves not only what you shouldn't say, but what you should say. For example, you shouldn't use profanity, complain, lie, or gossip. But you should speak up when you see injustice, encourage those who are down, and praise God every day. What comes out of your mouth most often? Ask a friend to make a mental list of your positive words and negative words. If you really want to stop the negative words, ask yourself before you speak: Is it true? Is it kind? Is it helpful?

GOD'S CHALLENGE

Don't use foul or abusive language. Let everything you say be good and helpful, so that your words will be an encouragement to those who hear them.   *Ephesians 4:29*

GIVING YOUR BEST

Why is it important to give our best to the Lord?

GOD'S RESPONSE

Be sure to set aside the best portions of the gifts given to you as your gifts to the LORD.   *Numbers 18:29*

When it was time for the harvest, Cain presented some of his crops as a gift to the LORD. Abel also brought a gift— the best of the firstborn lambs from his flock. The LORD accepted Abel and his gift, but he did not accept Cain and his gift.   *Genesis 4:3-5 (NLT2)*

G IVING YOUR BEST TO GOD shows the value you put on your relationship with him. If you are trying to get away with something less than the best, your motives reveal that God is not first in your life. Since your worship reflects your heart's condition, giving your best to God reflects what you think of him. Giving less than your best cheapens God's best gift to you—eternal life through the death and resurrection of his own Son, Jesus.

GOD'S PROMISE

Honor the LORD with your wealth and with the best part of everything your land produces. Then he will fill your barns with grain.   *Proverbs 3:9-10*

DISCONNECTION

When my life is not filled with the Holy Spirit, what can happen?

GOD'S RESPONSE

When you follow the desires of your sinful nature, your lives will produce these evil results: sexual immorality, impure thoughts, eagerness for lustful pleasure, idolatry, participation in demonic activities, hostility, quarreling, jealousy, outbursts of anger, selfish ambition, divisions, the feeling that everyone is wrong except those in your own little group, envy, drunkenness, wild parties, and other kinds of sin.   *Galatians 5:19-21*

THE HOLY SPIRIT cannot do his work in your life if you aren't connected to him. If you're not connected, you get no nourishment from him and you begin to follow your sinful desires. How much better to remain connected in your relationship with Jesus through the Holy Spirit and let him produce a great work in you. Get reconnected! Pray, read your Bible, worship with other believers, and listen to God. Your life will be so much happier.

GOD'S PROMISE

I am the vine; you are the branches. Those who remain in me, and I in them, will produce much fruit. For apart from me you can do nothing.   *John 15:5*

GOD'S ANGER

Will God ever lose his patience with me?

GOD'S RESPONSE

This made the LORD burn with anger against Israel, so he handed them over to marauders who stole their possessions. He sold them to their enemies all around, and they were no longer able to resist them. *Judges 2:14*

THE BIBLE CLEARLY EMPHASIZES a basic and powerful principle: following God leads to blessing, and abandoning God leads to misery. Without God as our shield, temptation and evil rush in unhindered. God loses patience only when you utterly fail to recognize his work in your life and abandon the godly principles that lead to his blessing. When God loses patience, you lose the mercy that you absolutely need to survive—and that is terrifying. God is very patient; he doesn't expect that you will be able to obey him perfectly—as humans we can't! All he asks is that you sincerely try to follow and obey him.

GOD'S PROMISE

You will experience all these blessings if you obey the LORD your God. . . . But if you refuse to listen to the LORD your God and do not obey . . . all these curses will come and overwhelm you. *Deuteronomy 28:2, 15*

REPENTANCE

Why is repentance necessary?

GOD'S RESPONSE

If my people who are called by my name will humble themselves and pray and seek my face and turn from their wicked ways, I will hear from heaven and will forgive their sins.   *2 Chronicles 7:14*

You will also perish unless you turn from your evil ways and turn to God.   *Luke 13:3*

HAVE YOU EVER SUDDENLY REALIZED that you were driving the wrong way on a one-way street? What you do next is much like the biblical idea of repentance. You make a U-turn and change your direction as fast as you can. Repentance is motivated by the realization that you have taken the wrong way in life. It is made complete when you admit your sin and make a commitment, with God's help, to change your life's direction. Repentance is essential for hope. Changing direction is necessary if we are to arrive at God's destination, heaven. Because of repentance, change is possible and we can experience God's fullest blessings.

GOD'S CHALLENGE

Turn from your sins and turn to God, so you can be cleansed of your sins.   *Acts 3:19*

APPROVAL

Do I have to earn God's approval?

GOD'S RESPONSE

We are made right in God's sight when we trust in Jesus Christ to take away our sins. And we all can be saved in this same way, no matter who we are or what we have done.   *Romans 3:22*

If they are saved by God's kindness, then it is not by their good works. For in that case, God's wonderful kindness would not be what it really is—free and undeserved. *Romans 11:6*

APPROVAL FROM GOD COMES when you ask Jesus Christ to forgive your sins and then accept him as Lord of your life. That is all! You simply need to believe that what God says in the Bible is true. You don't have to impress him first by accomplishing a list of good deeds. No matter how good you are, you do not win God's approval until your sins are forgiven. When he forgives your sins, he wipes them away as if you had never sinned.

GOD'S PROMISE

If you confess with your mouth that Jesus is Lord and believe in your heart that God raised him from the dead, you will be saved.   *Romans 10:9*

BOOMERANG

What are some of the things we do that come back to haunt us?

GOD'S RESPONSE

Jephthah said to them, "Aren't you the ones who hated me and drove me from my father's house? Why do you come to me now when you're in trouble?" *Judges 11:7*

I T HAS BEEN SAID, "Be careful how you treat others on your way up, because they are the same people you'll meet on your way down." In other words, life has cycles. Sometimes you are on the way up life's ladder and everything is going your way. You're at the top of your game. But there will also be times when life doesn't go your way, and you move down the ladder. You are struggling and need help—to find a job, to get out of financial trouble, to overcome a bad decision. It's ironic how often the very people you thought you didn't need at one point in life suddenly become important to you later. Treating all people with the grace, mercy, and kindness that God intends will usually cause you to be treated with that same grace, mercy, and kindness in your hour of need.

GOD'S CHALLENGE

You will always reap what you sow! *Galatians 6:7*

COMPROMISE

When is compromise dangerous?

GOD'S RESPONSE

Delilah pouted, "How can you tell me, 'I love you,' when you don't share your secrets with me?" . . . She tormented him with her nagging day after day until he was sick to death of it. Finally, Samson shared his secret with her.
Judges 16:15-17 (NLT2)

THE CRAFTY PHILISTINES knew they couldn't match Samson's brute strength, so they aimed at his weakness—his inability to stay away from seductive women. Temptation always strikes at our weak spots, not our strengths. Our weak spots are those areas we refuse to give over to God. They are joints in our armor at which the enemy takes aim, the areas in which we compromise our convictions for a few moments of pleasure. In those areas of weakness, we must ask God to cover our weaknesses with his strength. You must understand your weaknesses so you can arm yourself against Satan's attacks.

GOD'S PROMISE

God is faithful. He will keep the temptation from becoming so strong that you can't stand up against it.
1 Corinthians 10:13

BAD HABITS

How do I break a bad habit?

GOD'S RESPONSE

Do not let sin control the way you live; do not give in to its lustful desires. Do not let any part of your body become a tool of wickedness, to be used for sinning. Instead, give yourselves completely to God.   *Romans 6:12-13*

THE TERM BAD HABIT **BRINGS TO MIND** such things as smoking, alcohol, and drugs. But spreading gossip, complaining, or backbiting can become bad habits too. Worry as a bad habit can hurt us physically and spiritually. One of Satan's great lies is that we are victims who have no power to resist. The world teaches us that heredity, environment, and circumstances excuse us from responsibility. In actuality, our bad habits are spiritual battles, but God is more powerful than anything that seeks to control us. When we tap into his power through prayer and the support of fellow believers, God breaks the chains that hold us and sets us free.

GOD'S PROMISE

Don't you realize that whatever you choose to obey becomes your master? You can choose sin, which leads to death, or you can choose to obey God and receive his approval.   *Romans 6:16*

RIGHT LIVING

If the righteous suffer like everybody else,
why bother to live for God?

GOD'S RESPONSE

What's the use of living a righteous life?   *Job 35:3 (NLT2)*

Be strong and steady, always enthusiastic about the Lord's
work, for you know that nothing you do for the Lord is
ever useless.   *1 Corinthians 15:58*

I F THE REWARDS OF THIS EARTHLY LIFE were the only
thing to live for, then a "why bother" attitude would be
understandable. But there are two reasons why this perspective is mistaken. First, when we try to obey God, we put
ourselves in position to enjoy life the way God intended; our
relationships are more faithful, our lives are full of integrity,
and our consciences are clear. Second, this life is not all there
is. The Bible is clear that those who trust Jesus Christ for
forgiveness receive eternal life. Our faithfulness in this life
may or may not result in material prosperity, but the rewards
in heaven will be more than we could ever imagine.

GOD'S PROMISE

No eye has seen, no ear has heard, and no mind has
imagined what God has prepared for those who love
him.   *1 Corinthians 2:9*

FAITH

I know I'm supposed to have faith in God, but it seems so complicated. How can I ever have faith?

GOD'S RESPONSE

Jesus ignored their comments and said to Jairus, "Don't be afraid. Just trust me."   *Mark 5:36*

I do believe, but help me overcome my unbelief!
Mark 9:24 (NLT2)

Jesus prayed this prayer: "O Father, Lord of heaven and earth, thank you for hiding the truth from those who think themselves so wise and clever, and for revealing it to the childlike."   *Matthew 11:25*

WE OFTEN MAKE FAITH in God more complicated than it really is. Faith simply means trusting God to do what he has promised. The problem comes when we get confused over what exactly he has promised. A great use of your time is to study God's promises in the Bible. Then you will develop a childlike confidence in God as you see all the promises he has fulfilled and anticipate the ones yet to come.

GOD'S CHALLENGE

You believe because you have seen me. Blessed are those who haven't seen me and believe anyway.   *John 20:29*

GRACE

How does God's grace affect my daily life?

GOD'S RESPONSE

The LORD is merciful and gracious; he is slow to get angry and full of unfailing love.   *Psalm 103:8*

Let us come boldly to the throne of our gracious God. There we will receive his mercy, and we will find grace to help us when we need it.   *Hebrews 4:16*

G RACE IS ANOTHER WORD for the amazing kindness God showers on us, even when we do not deserve it. God's greatest act of kindness is to offer us salvation and eternal life even though we have ignored him, neglected him, and rebelled against him. God's grace sets you free from the power of sin when he forgives you, so that you can choose each day to overpower your sinful nature. God's grace changes your life because you understand what it feels like to be loved even when you have not loved in return. This should cause you to love others in the same way that God loves you. To whom can you be an example of God's grace today?

GOD'S PROMISE

We do not ask because we deserve help, but because you are so merciful.   *Daniel 9:18*

What does Jesus mean when he said we are the "salt of the earth"?

GOD'S RESPONSE

You are the salt of the earth. But what good is salt if it has lost its flavor?   *Matthew 5:13*

"Please, sir," the woman said, "give me some of that water! Then I'll never be thirsty again."   *John 4:15*

IN JESUS' DAY, salt was a valuable commodity. It was used for seasoning and as a preservative to keep meat from decaying. Jesus compares his followers to salt because we are to exert a preservative influence on the world around us. When we keep our hearts holy and pure and hold up the standards of living established by God's Word, we help preserve the world from total decay. How "salty" is your life? Do your words and actions have a preservative influence? Does your life make others thirsty for God?

GOD'S PROMISE

Be careful how you live among your unbelieving neighbors. Even if they accuse you of doing wrong, they will see your honorable behavior, and they will believe and give honor to God when he comes to judge the world.   *1 Peter 2:12*

CLEANSING

What does it really mean to be forgiven?

GOD'S RESPONSE

You are holy and blameless as you stand before him
without a single fault.   *Colossians 1:22*

No matter how deep the stain of your sins, I can remove it.
I can make you as clean as freshly fallen snow.   *Isaiah 1:18*

Oh, what joy for those whose disobedience is forgiven,
whose sins are put out of sight.   *Romans 4:7*

FORGIVENESS MEANS THAT GOD LOOKS at you as
though you have never sinned. When God forgives, he
doesn't sweep your sins under the carpet; instead, he completely removes them from existence and forgets them. If
you have confessed your sin, don't go through another day
under the weight of unnecessary guilt, because when you
sin again, he will forgive you if you sincerely ask him. You
can never ask too many times for God to forgive you—
this is his marvelous gift to you.

GOD'S PROMISE

He has removed our rebellious acts as far away from us
as the east is from the west.   *Psalm 103:12*

FORGIVENESS

There must be some sins that are too great to be forgiven. Can any sin be forgiven?

GOD'S RESPONSE

God has purchased our freedom with his blood and has forgiven all our sins.   *Colossians 1:14*

I assure you that any sin can be forgiven.   *Mark 3:28*

He forgives all my sins and heals all my diseases. . . . He has not punished us for all our sins, nor does he deal with us as we deserve. For his unfailing love toward those who fear him is as great as the height of the heavens above the earth. He has removed our rebellious acts as far away from us as the east is from the west.   *Psalm 103:3, 10-12*

FORGIVENESS IS NOT BASED ON the magnitude of the sin, but on the magnitude of the forgiver's love. No sin is too great for God's complete and unconditional forgiveness. The Bible does, however, mention one unforgivable sin—blasphemy against the Holy Spirit (see Mark 3:28-29 and Matthew 12:31). Only those who reject his forgiveness are out of its reach.

GOD'S PROMISE

Nothing can ever separate us from his love.   *Romans 8:38*

THANKS

How can I thank God for all he has done for me?

GOD'S RESPONSE

Great is the LORD! He is most worthy of praise! He is to be revered above all gods. The gods of other nations are merely idols, but the LORD made the heavens! *1 Chronicles 16:25-26*

Who can list the glorious miracles of the LORD? Who can ever praise him half enough? *Psalm 106:2*

Let us continually offer our sacrifice of praise to God by proclaiming the glory of his name. *Hebrews 13:15*

YOU CAN THANK GOD by offering him a sacrifice of praise. What does that mean? It means that you sacrifice, or give up something, to praise him instead. You might give up some sleep to get up early to praise him. Maybe you will give up some free time to spend time in prayer praising him. Perhaps you need to give up complaining to praise him for all he has done for you. Whatever it is for you, give God praise. He is worthy of it.

GOD'S CHALLENGE

It is good to give thanks to the LORD, to sing praises to the Most High. *Psalm 92:1*

DISCONTENTMENT

How do we lose our desire to obey God?

GOD'S RESPONSE

We must listen very carefully to the truth we have heard, or we may drift away from it.   *Hebrews 2:1*

Always give thanks for everything to God the Father in the name of our Lord Jesus Christ.   *Ephesians 5:20*

A T FIRST THE PEOPLE OF ISRAEL DID "everything as the Lord commanded." They had a real desire to obey God. How quickly that changed! Before long they were complaining and whining. We lose our desire to obey God when we start focusing on the little things that bother us and forget the greater blessings God sends. We think about what we don't have and stop appreciating all we do have. Are you appreciating all God has done for you with the same passion you once did? If not, take an inventory of your attitudes and start thanking God for each blessing.

GOD'S PROMISE

I will give you a new heart with new and right desires, and I will put a new spirit in you. I will take out your stony heart of sin and give you a new, obedient heart. And I will put my Spirit in you so you will obey my laws and do whatever I command.   *Ezekiel 36:27*

COMMITMENT

How can I show my commitment to God?

GOD'S RESPONSE

Give your bodies to God.   *Romans 12:1*

Jesus called out to them, "Come, be my disciples, and I will show you how to fish for people!" And they left their nets at once and went with him.   *Matthew 4:19-20*

If we are thrown into the blazing furnace, the God whom we serve is able to save us. . . . But even if he doesn't, Your Majesty can be sure that we will never serve your gods. *Daniel 3:17-18*

C OMMITMENT IS MORE than intellectual agreement; it involves giving your whole self—body, soul, emotions, and mind—to God for his use. Commitment requires a decision of the mind followed by an act of the will that you will follow through regardless of the difficulty or the cost. Commitment to God can be costly, but God promises to share great blessings with you if you are faithful in your commitment to him.

GOD'S PROMISE

If we are faithful to the end . . . we will share in all that belongs to Christ.   *Hebrews 3:14*

CELEBRATION

Does God have a problem with celebrating?

GOD'S RESPONSE

Nehemiah continued, "Go and celebrate with a feast of choice foods and sweet drinks, and share gifts of food with people who have nothing prepared." *Nehemiah 8:10*

Praise him with the tambourine and dancing; praise him with stringed instruments and flutes! *Psalm 150:4*

EZRA AND NEHEMIAH WERE SERIOUS, godly leaders of the people, but when they completed the walls it was time to celebrate, for God had helped them to succeed. In thanksgiving and dedication, the people listened to God's Word. This moment of joy and gladness was also a time for food and festivities—a holy party time—to remember, thank, praise, and honor God, and to dedicate themselves to him in a festive spirit with feasting and sharing. At Christmastime, birthdays, anniversaries, or any celebration, include these elements and you will be blessed beyond expectation.

GOD'S PROMISE

Let all who take refuge in you rejoice; let them sing joyful praises forever. Protect them, so all who love your name may be filled with joy. *Psalm 5:11*

GOD'S PLAN

How much does God direct the events of my life?

GOD'S RESPONSE

There is a time for everything, a season for every activity under heaven. . . . God has made everything beautiful for its own time.   *Ecclesiastes 3:1, 11*

THIS QUESTION MAY BEST BE ANSWERED toward the end of life, when you can look back and see how God has pieced together specific circumstances to form a master plan for you. You must be cautious about over-reacting to certain events in your life until you have seen God's entire plan for you. In the book of Ruth, we read about the troubles that came to Naomi. She thought that God had abandoned her, but God took those troubles and wove them into his grand plan for her, to the point that she became a direct ancestor of Jesus Christ! The events of your life may make little sense until you realize that God uses them to bring joy and purpose to those who love and obey him.

GOD'S PROMISE

These things I plan won't happen right away. Slowly, steadily, surely, the time approaches when the vision will be fulfilled. If it seems slow, wait patiently, for it will surely take place. It will not be delayed.   *Habakkuk 2:3*

HOLY SPIRIT

When and how do I receive the Holy Spirit?

GOD'S RESPONSE

Now you also have heard the truth, the Good News that God saves you. And when you believed in Christ, he identified you as his own by giving you the Holy Spirit, whom he promised long ago. The Spirit is God's guarantee that he will give us everything he promised and that he has purchased us to be his own people. This is just one more reason for us to praise our glorious God. *Ephesians 1:13-14*

G OD HAD LONG AGO PROMISED the Holy Spirit, but he didn't give it to the believers until after Jesus' resurrection and ascension to heaven. The presence of the Holy Spirit in your life guarantees that you will receive everything else God has promised. God gave you his Holy Spirit when you believed in Jesus Christ and accepted him as your Savior. Since the Spirit is now always present with you, every day is a new opportunity to receive his guidance and comfort. Will you listen to him and follow him today?

GOD'S PROMISE

God has actually given us his Spirit (not the world's spirit) so we can know the wonderful things God has freely given us. *1 Corinthians 2:12*

FLATTERY

How do I make sure I give a true compliment and not flattery?

GOD'S RESPONSE

Even when you do ask, you don't get it because your whole motive is wrong—you want only what will give you pleasure.   *James 4:3*

May the words of my mouth and the thoughts of my heart be pleasing to you, O LORD, my rock and my redeemer. *Psalm 19:14*

In the end, people appreciate frankness more than flattery.   *Proverbs 28:23*

THE DIFFERENCE BETWEEN A COMPLIMENT and flattery is found in the motivation behind the words. A sincere compliment is all about the other person, designed to build him or her up. Flattery is all about you, saying something nice to get you something in return. Never ignore your conscience—it will tell you if you are sincere.

GOD'S PROMISE

He died for us so that we can live with him forever. . . . So encourage each other and build each other up, just as you are already doing.   *1 Thessalonians 5:10-11*

BURNOUT

What is burnout?

GOD'S RESPONSE

[Elijah] sat down under a solitary broom tree and prayed that he might die. "I have had enough, LORD," he said. *1 Kings 19:4*

I am exhausted and completely crushed. My groans come from an anguished heart.   *Psalm 38:8*

B URNOUT IS THE EMOTIONAL exhaustion that comes when reality persistently falls short of our expectations. Elijah was convinced that his spiritual victory would transform Ahab's heart and change the spiritual climate of Israel, but instead of implementing reforms, Ahab threatened Elijah's life. Just at the moment of triumph, Elijah grew depressed and quit—classic signs of burnout, which can be a particular problem for Christians. God's power is limitless, but we still live in a fallen world. Learn to recognize burnout before it overwhelms you and renders you ineffective for serving God.

GOD'S PROMISE

Don't get tired of doing what is good. Don't get discouraged and give up, for we will reap a harvest of blessing at the appropriate time.   *Galatians 6:9*

BURNOUT

How can I avoid burnout?

GOD'S RESPONSE

The angel of the LORD . . . touched him and said, "Get up and eat some more, for there is a long journey ahead of you." So he got up and ate and drank.   *1 Kings 19:7-8*

E LIJAH'S EXPERIENCE SUGGESTS three steps to beating burnout. (1) Take care of your body. A healthy diet and regular exercise are essential. (2) Connect with other people. Elijah thought he was the only person in Israel still faithful to God, but there were actually 7,000 of them! When you isolate yourself or start thinking, I'm the only one who cares about this cause, you're in trouble. (3) Do God's work today. God gave Elijah specific steps that the prophet could achieve. Work at the tasks God has set before you and leave the results to God. Realize it's not up to you to do everything.

GOD'S PROMISE

Even youths will become exhausted, and young men will give up. But those who wait on the LORD will find new strength. They will fly high on wings like eagles. They will run and not grow weary. They will walk and not faint.   *Isaiah 40:30-31*

DANGER

What can be dangerous about power?

GOD'S RESPONSE

O Egypt, to which of the trees of Eden will you compare your strength and glory? You, too, will be brought down to the pit with all these other nations. You will lie there among the outcasts who have died by the sword. This will be the fate of Pharaoh and all his teeming hordes. I, the Sovereign LORD, have spoken! *Ezekiel 31:18*

POWER IS INTOXICATING—with it comes recognition, control, and often wealth. Each of these feeds pride, and pride leads us away from God and into sin. This is why power so often corrupts. If you are in a position of power or authority, two things will help you use it wisely: accountability and service. When you have to explain your motives to others, you will be more careful in what you do and say. When you determine to serve others with your power rather than be served, you will gain great support and loyalty from those in your care.

GOD'S PROMISE

The arrogance of all people will be brought low. Their pride will lie in the dust. The LORD alone will be exalted! *Isaiah 2:17*

PERSPECTIVE

How can I praise God when life is difficult?

GOD'S RESPONSE

No matter what happens, always be thankful, for this is God's will for you who belong to Christ Jesus. *1 Thessalonians 5:18*

LIFE CAN BE DIFFICULT for a number of reasons. You may be experiencing the consequences of your own sin, you may be suffering because of someone else's sin, you may be caught in circumstances that are no one's fault but are nonetheless unfortunate, God may be testing your faith, or you may be a target for Satan who wants to disrupt your godly influence. In any of these tough circumstances there is reason to praise God. He redeems our mistakes, teaches us wisdom through adversity, promises to help us through tough times, and guarantees eternal life free from suffering for all who are his followers. A God who redeems all trouble is a God worthy of praise.

GOD'S PROMISE

He will remove all of their sorrows, and there will be no more death or sorrow or crying or pain.   *Revelation 21:4*

BATTLES

Why does it seem like someone or something is always fighting me?

GOD'S RESPONSE

We are not fighting against people made of flesh and blood, but against the evil rulers and authorities of the unseen world, against those mighty powers of darkness who rule this world, and against wicked spirits in the heavenly realms. *Ephesians 6:12*

SATAN IS ALIVE AND ACTIVE, and his legions of demons are always on the attack. A battle rages in the spiritual realm—a battle you can't see but one that you will experience if you seek to serve God. You need God's power, not your own, to stand strong and not allow temptations to draw you away. Most of all, since you do not always know or understand the evil that is threatening you, you need God's power to give you strength to face an unknown enemy. Have peace that God's knowledge and power will save you in battle.

GOD'S PROMISE

The God of peace will soon crush Satan under your feet. *Romans 16:20*

How powerful is Satan?

GOD'S RESPONSE

Satan was there at the angel's right hand, accusing Jeshua of many things. And the LORD said to Satan, "I, the LORD, reject your accusations, Satan."   *Zechariah 3:1-2*

A T ONE TIME THE MOST BEAUTIFUL of all the angels, Satan became proud, sinned against God, and was cast out of heaven (Revelation 12:9). As a created being, Satan has definite limitations—for example, Satan does not share God's attributes of omniscience (all-knowing), omnipresence (being everywhere at all times) and omnipotence (all-powerful). He is God's enemy, but he is not God's equal. As God's enemy, he tries to prevent people from believing in God. For those who are already believers, Satan's ultimate weapon is division. If Satan can get God's people to fight with one another, he will have no worries about God's Kingdom advancing. Although God has allowed Satan certain power and influence to tempt and even destroy, Satan will not be the final victor.

GOD'S PROMISE

Then the Devil, who betrayed them, was thrown into the lake of fire that burns with sulfur.   *Revelation 20:10*

Is spiritual warfare a reality?

GOD'S RESPONSE

He said, "Don't be afraid, Daniel. Since the first day you began to pray for understanding and to humble yourself before your God, your request has been heard in heaven. I have come in answer to your prayer. But for twenty-one days the spirit prince of the kingdom of Persia blocked my way. Then Michael, one of the archangels, came to help me." *Daniel 10:12-13*

Jesus was led out into the wilderness by the Holy Spirit to be tempted there by the Devil. *Matthew 4:1*

THE BIBLE CLEARLY TEACHES that human beings are involved in a spiritual battle. Far from excluding you from this spiritual battle, faith puts you right in the middle of it. You are in a battle for your soul. You must recognize that and arm yourself, or you will be defeated.

GOD'S CHALLENGE

We are not fighting against people made of flesh and blood, but against the evil rulers and authorities of the unseen world, against those mighty powers of darkness who rule this world, and against wicked spirits in the heavenly realms. *Ephesians 6:12*

SPIRITUAL WARFARE

How does spiritual warfare affect me?

GOD'S RESPONSE

Be careful! Watch out for attacks from the Devil, your great enemy. He prowls around like a roaring lion, looking for some victim to devour. Take a firm stand against him, and be strong in your faith.   *1 Peter 5:8-9*

THE PURPOSE OF EVIL IS TO DEFY GOD and wear down believers until they are led into sin. This gives Satan pleasure and greater power over the earth. Therefore, you must be alert at all times for both the sneak attacks and the frontal attacks of the evil one. He will try to distort God's Word, hoping to make you doubt its integrity and, therefore, to question God's will and intentions for you. Eventually, God will take away and destroy the power of evil for all time. Until that day, we overcome evil by choosing to obey God.

GOD'S CHALLENGE

Don't let anyone lead you astray with empty philosophy and high-sounding nonsense that come from human thinking and from the evil powers of this world, and not from Christ.   *Colossians 2:8*

Can God really accomplish what seems impossible?

GOD'S RESPONSE

Jesus looked at them intently and said, "Humanly speaking, it is impossible. But with God everything is possible." *Matthew 19:26*

For nothing is impossible with God. *Luke 1:37*

The LORD said to Moses, "Is there any limit to my power? Now you will see whether or not my word comes true!" *Numbers 11:23*

TOO OFTEN OUR OWN LIMITATIONS cause us to doubt God's ability to work through us. Too often people make excuses for why they think things won't happen instead of thinking about how they might happen, especially when almighty God is involved. The next time you think a promise from God is impossible, or you are facing a seemingly impossible problem, look at the issue again from God's perspective and ask him to do the impossible in you!

GOD'S PROMISE

"Abba, Father," he said, "everything is possible for you." *Mark 14:36*

IMPOSSIBILITY

What if a task I need to complete looks impossible?

GOD'S RESPONSE

This is what the LORD Almighty says: Once again old men and women will walk Jerusalem's streets with a cane and sit together in the city squares. And the streets of the city will be filled with boys and girls at play. . . . All this may seem impossible to you now, a small and discouraged remnant of God's people. But do you think this is impossible for me, the LORD Almighty? *Zechariah 8:4-6*

THE TEMPLE IN JERUSALEM STILL NEEDED to be rebuilt after long years of exile, but the people weren't motivated to finish it. God gave Zechariah a vision of the city of Jerusalem filled once again with joyful people, and that vision, in turn, motivated the people to complete their task. If a tough task hangs over you, ask God to give you a vision for the finished project and a sense of the joy you will have when the job is done.

GOD'S CHALLENGE

This is what the LORD Almighty says: Take heart and finish the task! *Zechariah 8:9*

GOD'S PROMISES

God's promises seem too impossible for me;
how could they ever come true in my life?

GOD'S RESPONSE

Then the LORD said to Abraham, . . . "Is anything too hard
for the LORD? About a year from now, just as I told you,
I will return, and Sarah will have a son." . . . Then the LORD
did exactly what he had promised. . . . It all happened at the
time God had said it would. *Genesis 18:13-14; 21:1-2*

M AYBE THE PROMISES OF God look impossible in
your life—you feel you've messed up, missed your
opportunities, or have gotten too old. God asks you what
he asked Abraham: "Is anything too hard for the Lord?"
The great thing about God's promises is that the burden
is on God. It's not your job to worry about how he will
fulfill them, but to live faithfully and be open to his working in your life. He will lead you places you might never
expect. Often it is our own skepticism that prevents us
from stepping out in faith into one of God's miracles.

GOD'S PROMISE

Now that you belong to Christ, you are the true children
of Abraham. You are his heirs, and now all the promises
God gave to him belong to you. *Galatians 3:29*

SECOND CHANCES

I've been running from God all my life.
Is it possible for God to use me now?

GOD'S RESPONSE

The LORD gave this message to Jonah son of Amittai: "Get up and go to the great city of Nineveh! Announce my judgment against it because I have seen how wicked its people are." But Jonah got up and went in the opposite direction in order to get away from the LORD. . . . Then the LORD spoke to Jonah a second time: "Get up and go to the great city of Nineveh, and deliver the message of judgment I have given you."   *Jonah 1:1-3; 3:1-2*

N O MATTER HOW OFTEN YOU'VE RUN from God or avoided him, he knew where you were. Jonah tried to run, but he ended up running right back to God—by way of a tumultuous ocean and a giant fish. Your God, the God of Jonah, is a God of second chances. When you stop running, you can be sure that God wants to use you to accomplish something significant for him. Don't be surprised if your experience of running from God just happens to have perfectly prepared you for the job he has for you to do.

GOD'S PROMISE

He will rescue you again and again so that no evil can touch you.   *Job 5:19*

RESISTANCE

With so much evil in the world, is it really possible to resist?

GOD'S RESPONSE

Elijah the prophet walked up to the altar and prayed, "O Lord, God of Abraham, Isaac, and Jacob, prove today that you are God in Israel and that I am your servant. Prove that I have done all this at your command. . . . Immediately the fire of the Lord flashed down from heaven. . . . When the people saw it, they fell on their faces and cried out, "The Lord is God! The Lord is God!" *1 Kings 18:36, 38-39*

I F YOU'RE FEELING OVERWHELMED, you may be taking too large a perspective. Let God worry about all the injustice in the world; you just need to find one small injustice and start there. The world is filled with evil, and you are here to be a light in the darkness. Even a small candle can lighten a dark room. As you minister, you may find that others gain the courage to join you, and you can begin to broaden your perspective.

GOD'S PROMISE

Be strong and courageous! Do not be afraid or discouraged. For the Lord your God is with you wherever you go. *Joshua 1:9*

ODDS

How can I expect victory when the odds are stacked high against me?

GOD'S RESPONSE

When King Hezekiah heard their report, he tore his clothes and put on sackcloth and went into the Temple of the LORD to pray. . . . "O LORD our God, rescue us from his power." *2 Kings 19:1, 19*

The LORD sent an angel who destroyed the Assyrian army. *2 Chronicles 32:21*

THE ODDS WERE DEFINITELY STACKED against the little nation of Judah. The mighty Assyrian army had already destroyed every nation in its path . . . and Judah was next. So King Hezekiah did the only thing he could do—he went to the Temple and prayed. Assyria's mighty army was no match for God. You, too, will succeed at whatever God has called you to if you humbly and faithfully follow him, no matter how much the odds seem stacked against you.

GOD'S PROMISE

This is what the LORD says: Do not be disturbed by this blasphemous speech against me from the Assyrian king's messengers. Listen! I myself will move against him. *2 Kings 19:6-7*

BURDENS

What can I do when my job is too much to handle?

GOD'S RESPONSE

You're going to wear yourself out—and the people, too. This job is too heavy a burden for you to handle all by yourself. . . . Find some capable, honest men who fear God and hate bribes. Appoint them as judges over groups of one thousand, one hundred, fifty, and ten. These men can serve the people, resolving all the ordinary cases. . . . They will help you carry the load.   *Exodus 18:18, 21-22*

I F YOUR JOB IS OVERBURDENING YOU, then you need to do whatever you can to share the load. It does mean sharing responsibility and sharing credit, but it also means that you won't be wearing yourself out with nothing left for anyone else—including God. You'll be amazed at how much lighter a burden is when it is shared. Sharing your work with others will allow you to make the most valuable use of your time for others and for God.

GOD'S CHALLENGE

Two people can accomplish more than twice as much as one. . . . If one person falls, the other can reach out and help. But people who are alone when they fall are in real trouble. . . . Three are even better, for a triple-braided cord is not easily broken.   *Ecclesiastes 4:9-10, 12*

CONFLICT

What if I'm involved in a conflict that seems impossible to resolve?

GOD'S RESPONSE

After some time Paul said to Barnabas, "Let's return to each city where we previously preached the word of the Lord, to see how the new believers are getting along." Barnabas agreed and wanted to take along John Mark. But Paul disagreed strongly. . . . Their disagreement over this was so sharp that they separated.   *Acts 15:36-39*

J ESUS SAID WE SHOULD make every effort to resolve conflicts with one another. If both parties have the same end goal, see if you can compromise on how to get there. Sometimes, you may have to agree to disagree. Do so with respect and love, honoring God even in your disagreement. God will then use both your efforts for good. Paul and Barnabas disagreed so sharply that they decided to separate, yet God used this separation to double their effort and create two strong missionary teams. God can work his will through conflicts in ways you may not see.

GOD'S PROMISE

God blesses those who work for peace, for they will be called the children of God.   *Matthew 5:9*

PREPARATION

How does God prepare me for what he has in store for me?

GOD'S RESPONSE

When her son was born, they named him Samson. And the LORD blessed him as he grew up.   *Judges 13:24*

Put on all of God's armor so that you will be able to stand firm against all strategies and tricks of the Devil. *Ephesians 6:11*

AS SOON AS SAMSON WAS BORN, God's spirit began to work in him to prepare Samson for a unique job. Samson was supposed to do his part in return—listen for God's voice, obey his clear instructions, and act on the opportunities God would bring to him. Sadly, Samson didn't do this and never reached his full potential. What is the Spirit of the Lord preparing you for? The key to recognizing his work in your life is first to obey God's clear instructions for living as found in the Bible. If you follow God, your life will go in the right direction.

GOD'S PROMISE

Study this Book of the Law continually. Meditate on it day and night so you may be sure to obey all that is written in it. Only then will you succeed.   *Joshua 1:8*

FAITH

How do I handle instructions from God that seem to make no sense?

GOD'S RESPONSE

Make a boat from resinous wood and seal it with tar, inside and out. . . . Look! I am about to cover the earth with a flood that will destroy every living thing. Everything on earth will die! But I solemnly swear to keep you safe in the boat, with your wife and your sons and their wives. *Genesis 6:14, 17-18*

TRUSTING GOD MEANS OBEYING HIM, even when it doesn't make sense to you, because you have unshakable confidence in his character. God told Noah to build a boat in the middle of the desert. It didn't make sense—until those first big drops of rain started to spatter in the dust! Noah obeyed out of faith, not logic. He obeyed because he trusted God to do what he said he would do. The next time your faith feels out of place in a world oblivious to God's warnings and commands, remember that the ark was built on obedient trust.

GOD'S PROMISE

If you obey the commands of the LORD your God and walk in his ways, the LORD will establish you as his holy people. *Deuteronomy 28:9*

HEROES

Most heroes are those who persevere against hardship. How can I emulate such people?

GOD'S RESPONSE

All of these people we have mentioned received God's approval because of their faith, yet none of them received all that God had promised. For God had far better things in mind for us that would also benefit them, for they can't receive the prize at the end of the race until we finish the race.   *Hebrews 11:39-40*

GOD'S HEROES HANG ON TO THEIR FAITH in him no matter what happens. The Bible is full of examples of people who never stopped trusting God even when they were mocked, persecuted, or killed for their faith. God may not ask you to be a martyr for him, but is your faith strong enough to endure even a little derision or scorn? Determine to be faithful to God no matter what.

GOD'S PROMISE

We give great honor to those who endure under suffering. Job is an example of a man who endured patiently. From his experience we see how the Lord's plan finally ended in good, for he is full of tenderness and mercy.   *James 5:11*

COMMITMENT

How do I stay committed to God despite pressures to do otherwise?

GOD'S RESPONSE

Nebuchadnezzar said to them, "Is it true, Shadrach, Meshach, and Abednego, that you refuse to serve my gods or to worship the gold statue? . . . If you refuse, you will be thrown immediately into the blazing furnace. What god will be able to rescue you from my power then?"

Shadrach, Meshach, and Abednego replied, . . . "If we are thrown into the blazing furnace, the God whom we serve is able to save us. . . . [But] we will never serve your gods or worship the gold statue you have set up." *Daniel 3:14-18*

THESE THREE HEBREW MEN KNEW that following God could cost them their lives. Many of us might simply have pretended to bow down while praying to God secretly in our hearts. However, there are times when a public statement of faith may be necessary. At these times it makes more sense to focus on what you will gain through commitment to God than on what you will lose by compromising.

GOD'S CHALLENGE

Take a firm stand against [the devil], and be strong in your faith. *1 Peter 5:9*

ENDURANCE

How can I become stronger in my faith?

GOD'S RESPONSE

Whenever trouble comes your way, let it be an opportunity for joy. For when your faith is tested, your endurance has a chance to grow. *James 1:2-3*

Be strong and courageous, and do the work. Don't be afraid or discouraged by the size of the task, for the LORD God, my God, is with you. He will not fail you or forsake you. *1 Chronicles 28:20*

J UST BECAUSE YOU ARE FOLLOWING GOD in something doesn't make it easy. In fact, the more important a task is, the more Satan will throw up roadblocks. If you know that God is leading you in a certain direction, don't give up just because the going gets tough. If anything, that should tell you that you are headed in the right direction. Keep moving forward boldly and your faith will be strengthened as you obey God in the daily choices of your life. When you do, you will be able to step out in stronger faith whenever God calls you.

GOD'S PROMISE

The LORD is for me, so I will not be afraid. What can mere mortals do to me? *Psalm 118:6*

ROLE MODEL

Is it my responsibility to be a good role model?

GOD'S RESPONSE

Be an example to all believers in what you teach, in the way you live, in your love, your faith, and your purity. *1 Timothy 4:12*

You yourself must be an example to them by doing good deeds of every kind.   *Titus 2:7*

L IKE FATHER LIKE SON." "The apple doesn't fall far from the tree." These are phrases we smile at that also carry an enduring element of truth. We tend to be amazingly similar to our parents because they have been our models of how to think and act. Judah was one of the ringleaders in selling his brother into slavery; he shouldn't have been surprised when his sons treated others cruelly. What you say and do will be copied by those closest to you, which gives you the potential for passing on great good or great evil. If you have had poor role models, determine to stop the cycle and to influence those around you to follow God with passion and purpose.

GOD'S CHALLENGE

Mark out a straight path for your feet. Then those who follow you, though they are weak and lame, will not stumble and fall but will become strong.   *Hebrews 12:13*

How is it possible for me to do anything significant for God when I have so few resources?

GOD'S RESPONSE

Jesus soon saw a great crowd of people climbing the hill, looking for him. Turning to Philip, he asked, "Philip, where can we buy bread to feed all these people?" ... Philip replied, "It would take a small fortune to feed them!" Then Andrew, Simon Peter's brother, spoke up. "There's a young boy here with five barley loaves and two fish. But what good is that with this huge crowd?" *John 6:5, 7-9*

I N FOOTBALL, a wide receiver is sometimes asked to run a deep route simply to clear space for the primary receiver running a shorter route. Even though it takes very few resources for the first receiver to run straight down the field, his job is still necessary for the play to work. Don't feel useless or insulted by the little tasks in life. If you avoid them, you may miss out on something big that God is doing.

GOD'S PROMISE

To those who use well what they are given, even more will be given, and they will have an abundance. But from those who are unfaithful, even what little they have will be taken away. *Matthew 25:29*

OBSTACLES

How do I proceed when a task seems impossible?

GOD'S RESPONSE

Sanballat was very angry when he learned that we were rebuilding the wall. He flew into a rage and mocked the Jews, saying . . . "What does this bunch of poor, feeble Jews think they are doing?"   *Nehemiah 4:1-2*

When our enemies and the surrounding nations heard [the wall was finished], they were frightened and humiliated. They realized that this work had been done with the help of our God.   *Nehemiah 6:16*

SOMETIMES YOU'LL NEED TO BE CREATIVE to get around obstacles. Sometimes you'll need to ignore them and sometimes you'll need to pray your way through them. Seemingly impossible tasks—such as rebuilding the wall of Jerusalem—are often accomplished by laying one small stone at a time. When God wants a job done, it will get done regardless of the obstacles.

GOD'S PROMISE

I am sure that God, who began the good work within you, will continue his work until it is finally finished on that day when Christ Jesus comes back again. *Philippians 1:6*

OPPOSITION

What should I do when I encounter opposition because I follow God?

GOD'S RESPONSE

All the kings west of the Jordan . . . quickly combined their armies to fight against Joshua and the Israelites. *Joshua 9:1-2*

As long as the king sought the LORD, God gave him success. *2 Chronicles 26:5*

WHEN THE KINGS OF southern Canaan formed an alliance against the Israelites, Joshua did not let them intimidate him. He knew that following God brings victory in our lives and also stirs greater opposition. Expect this opposition and resolve to follow God with even greater commitment after a victory. Joshua and his leaders let their guard down after victory and were deceived by the enemy. We are most vulnerable in the afterglow of success, the most invincible when utterly dependent on God.

GOD'S PROMISE

God blesses you when you are mocked and persecuted and lied about because you are my followers. Be happy about it! Be very glad! For a great reward awaits you in heaven. *Matthew 5:11-12*

OPPOSITION

How should I respond to opposition?

GOD'S RESPONSE

I come to you for protection, O LORD my God. Save me from my persecutors—rescue me! *Psalm 7:1*

Don't repay evil for evil. Don't retaliate when people say unkind things about you. Instead, pay them back with a blessing. That is what God wants you to do, and he will bless you for it. *1 Peter 3:9*

I say, love your enemies! Pray for those who persecute you! *Matthew 5:44*

AT TIMES, YOUR BEST RESPONSE to opposition is no response at all. By repaying evil for evil, you stoop to fighting on the opposition's terms and you cut yourself off from God's righteous power. Try to love and pray for those who oppose you. No matter how much opposition you experience, continue doing right, trust in God, and keep yourself tapped into God's strong power and protection.

GOD'S PROMISE

If you are suffering according to God's will, keep on doing what is right, and trust yourself to the God who made you, for he will never fail you. *1 Peter 4:19*

SPEAKING UP

*When is it appropriate to speak up for what
is right?*

GOD'S RESPONSE

Speak up for those who cannot speak for themselves;
ensure justice for those who are perishing. Yes, speak up
for the poor and helpless, and see that they get justice.
Proverbs 31:8-9

T HERE ARE SITUATIONS in which it is appropriate for
you to speak up. When you can, it is your duty to
call people to act against injustices in the world, especially
on behalf of those who cannot speak for themselves. You
are also called to speak up when you know that a friend
or family member is disobeying God or hurting others.
In all you do, make it a priority to get the right message
about God across to others who may not understand or
know any better.

GOD'S CHALLENGE

If a person is ashamed of me and my message . . . I,
the Son of Man, will be ashamed of that person when
I return in the glory of my Father with the holy angels.
Mark 8:38

RETIREMENT

What does the Bible say about retirement?

GOD'S RESPONSE

The LORD also instructed Moses, "This is the rule the Levites must follow: They must begin serving in the Tabernacle at the age of twenty-five, and they must retire at the age of fifty. After retirement they may assist their fellow Levites by performing guard duty at the Tabernacle, but they may not officiate in the service."   *Numbers 8:23-26*

W E SHOULD NOT ASSUME that fifty is the age the Bible suggests for all workers to retire! This is one of the few references to retirement in the Bible. Possibly this was to encourage younger Levites to grow into positions of responsibility. Nowhere does the Bible say that retirement means stopping work and service altogether; rather, it changes how we work and serve. Few things are more important than developing strong leaders in the church. At times, older leaders must shift to mentoring new leaders for the future strength of the church.

GOD'S CHALLENGE

Among you it should be quite different. Whoever wants to be a leader among you must be your servant, and whoever wants to be first must be the slave of all.
Mark 10:43-44

CHALLENGES

How should challenges shape my life?

GOD'S RESPONSE

I have been following the plan spoken of in the Scriptures, where it says, "Those who have never been told about him will see, and those who have never heard of him will understand." In fact, my visit to you has been delayed so long because I have been preaching in these places. *Romans 15:21-22*

Dear brothers and sisters, whenever trouble comes your way, let it be an opportunity for joy. *James 1:2*

C HALLENGES KEEP YOU from being comfortable and satisfied with the status quo. They force you to follow God's leading into uncharted waters. Facing dangers of various sorts is part of the challenge of serving God in all things. These challenges reveal God's grace and power, develop your endurance, and teach you to better exercise the gifts God has given you. Paul's vision to preach the gospel in new places continually drove him to new challenges and therefore to greater growth in his relationship with God.

GOD'S PROMISE

Commit everything you do to the LORD. Trust him, and he will help you. *Psalm 37:5*

CHALLENGES

What are some of the ways God challenges me?

GOD'S RESPONSE

Jesus felt genuine love for this man as he looked at him. "You lack only one thing," he told him. "Go and sell all you have and give the money to the poor, and you will have treasure in heaven. Then come, follow me." At this, the man's face fell, and he went sadly away because he had many possessions. *Mark 10:21-22*

Put me on trial, LORD, and cross-examine me. Test my motives and affections. *Psalm 26:2*

G OD WANTS YOU to examine your heart, that is, to test your motives to discover what you value most. Another part of the "heart test" is how you react to problems that interrupt your life. Do they drive you to ask God for help, or do you usually try to solve them without even thinking about God? How would you respond if God asked you to give away everything you have to follow him? These are some ways that God challenges us. How are you handling the test?

GOD'S PROMISE

I will give you a new heart with new and right desires, and I will put a new spirit in you. *Ezekiel 36:26*

Why is it important for me to give thanks to the Lord?

GOD'S RESPONSE

Giving thanks is a sacrifice that truly honors me. If you keep to my path, I will reveal to you the salvation of God. *Psalm 50:23*

All of your works will thank you, LORD, and your faithful followers will bless you.   *Psalm 145:10*

Since everything God created is good, we should not reject any of it. We may receive it gladly, with thankful hearts.   *1 Timothy 4:4*

A THANKFUL HEART HONORS GOD for what he has done and recognizes his work, blessing, mercy, and provision in your life. A thankful heart gives you a positive attitude because it keeps you focused on all God is doing for you, not on what you think you lack. This prepares you for life's challenges and for faithfulness to God in the midst of challenges. Make thanksgiving a part of your prayer time every day.

GOD'S PROMISE

Give thanks to the LORD, for he is good! His faithful love endures forever.   *1 Chronicles 16:34*

THANKFULNESS

How can I show my thankfulness to the Lord?

GOD'S RESPONSE

I will thank you, Lord, with all my heart; I will tell of all the marvelous things you have done.   *Psalm 9:1*

It is good to give thanks to the Lord, to sing praises to the Most High. It is good to proclaim your unfailing love in the morning, your faithfulness in the evening. *Psalm 92:1-2*

When I learn your righteous laws, I will thank you by living as I should!   *Psalm 119:7*

THERE ARE MANY WAYS to show your thankfulness to the Lord—through praise, prayer, singing, worship, giving, obedience, and service. Like you, God loves to hear a simple "thank you."

GOD'S CHALLENGE

Give thanks to the Lord and proclaim his greatness.
Let the whole world know what he has done.
1 Chronicles 16:8

THANKFULNESS

What should I thank God for?

GOD'S RESPONSE

I will thank the LORD with all my heart as I meet with his godly people. How amazing are the deeds of the LORD! All who delight in him should ponder them.   *Psalm 111:1-2*

I will give thanks to your name for your unfailing love and faithfulness, because your promises are backed by all the honor of your name.   *Psalm 138:2*

Thank God for his Son—a gift too wonderful for words! *2 Corinthians 9:15*

THERE ARE SO MANY THINGS to thank God for— salvation, faith, love, heaven, miracles, food, other believers, family, work, nature, laughter, his unfailing faithfulness, his honor, his goodness, his Son . . . in fact, you can give thanks for everything good!

GOD'S CHALLENGE

Let your roots grow down into him and draw up nourishment from him, so you will grow in faith, strong and vigorous in the truth you were taught. Let your lives overflow with thanksgiving for all he has done. *Colossians 2:7*

THANKFULNESS

How can I show my thankfulness to others?

GOD'S RESPONSE

"Oh, thank you, sir!" she exclaimed.   *1 Samuel 1:18*

He fell face down on the ground at Jesus' feet, thanking him for what he had done. This man was a Samaritan. *Luke 17:16*

I have never stopped thanking God for you. I pray for you constantly, asking God, the glorious Father of our Lord Jesus Christ, to give you spiritual wisdom and understanding, so that you might grow in your knowledge of God.   *Ephesians 1:16-17*

THERE ARE SO MANY WAYS to show your thankfulness to others—a word of thanks, a smile, a note, a meal, a gift, a prayer, a recommendation. To whom can you say thank you today?

GOD'S PROMISE

How we thank God, who gives us victory over sin and death through Jesus Christ our Lord!
1 Corinthians 15:57

THANKFULNESS

How can I be thankful even in the tough times?

GOD'S RESPONSE

Don't worry about anything; instead, pray about everything. Tell God what you need, and thank him for all he has done.   *Philippians 4:6*

No matter what happens, always be thankful, for this is God's will for you who belong to Christ Jesus. *1 Thessalonians 5:18*

WHILE IT IS HARD TO BE THANKFUL for the tough times, you can be thankful in them. Our outlook on life determines how we view our problems. If we see them only as problems, we will usually develop an attitude of bitterness, cynicism, and hopelessness. If we see them as a crucible for strengthening our character and convictions, then we are better able to rise above them, and even thank God for how they are refining our lives.

GOD'S PROMISE

Since we are his children, we will share his treasures—for everything God gives to his Son, Christ, is ours, too. But if we are to share his glory, we must also share his suffering. Yet what we suffer now is nothing compared to the glory he will give us later.   *Romans 8:17-18*

PURIFICATION

Why do tough times come? What value do they have in my life?

GOD'S RESPONSE

Fire tests the purity of silver and gold, but the LORD tests the heart.   *Proverbs 17:3*

Remove the dross from silver, and the sterling will be ready for the silversmith.   *Proverbs 25:4*

He will sit and judge like a refiner of silver, watching closely as the dross is burned away.   *Malachi 3:3*

AS PRECIOUS METALS ARE REFINED BY FIRE, so your life, which is precious to God, is refined and purified in the fire of adversity. It is only through refining that the impurities are removed. When the liquid metal is completely purified, the refiner's image appears on its surface. Likewise, through suffering, God's image will appear more and more clearly in you.

GOD'S PROMISE

I will bring that group through the fire and make them pure, just as gold and silver are refined and purified by fire. They will call on my name, and I will answer them. I will say, "These are my people," and they will say, "The LORD is our God."   *Zechariah 13:9*

TROUBLE

How can I avoid trouble?

GOD'S RESPONSE

If you keep your mouth shut, you will stay out of trouble.
Proverbs 21:23

Blessed are those who have a tender conscience, but the stubborn are headed for serious trouble.   *Proverbs 28:14*

The trustworthy will get a rich reward. But the person who wants to get rich quick will only get into trouble.
Proverbs 28:20

THERE ARE TWO KINDS OF TROUBLE—trouble that you cause because of a mistake, a bad decision, or an act of sin, and trouble that invades your life through no fault of your own. The first kind of trouble can usually be avoided through good planning and godly living. The second kind of trouble cannot usually be avoided, but God promises to help us through it and to eliminate it forever one day. You won't always be able to avoid trouble, but you can keep from looking for it!

GOD'S PROMISE

The power of the life-giving Spirit has freed you through Christ Jesus from the power of sin that leads to death.
Romans 8:2

ABSENCE

Is God absent in my times of trouble?

GOD'S RESPONSE

O LORD, how long will you forget me? Forever? How long will you look the other way? How long must I struggle with anguish in my soul, with sorrow in my heart every day? How long will my enemy have the upper hand?   *Psalm 13:1-2*

GOD NEVER PROMISED that by believing in him your life would be free from trouble. In fact, he promised that by believing him, your life would probably have trouble because you have declared sides and now you have Satan as an enemy. Knowing this truth does not make your troubles easier, but because God predicted this trouble and knows the events of your life before they occur, you can move through troubling times without fear. When you face times of suffering, sorrow, or loneliness, remember that God is close beside you and knows that the outcome will be victory for you.

GOD'S PROMISE

Even when I walk through the dark valley of death, I will not be afraid, for you are close beside me. Your rod and your staff protect and comfort me.   *Psalm 23:4*

How can I use my own personal experiences to tell others about God?

GOD'S RESPONSE

You will be able to tell wonderful stories to your children and grandchildren about the marvelous things I am doing. *Exodus 10:2*

I will teach you hidden lessons from our past—stories we have heard and know, stories our ancestors handed down to us. We will not hide these truths from our children but will tell the next generation about the glorious deeds of the Lord. *Psalm 78:2-4*

IF BIBLE STORIES ABOUT PEOPLE we've never met teach us about God, how much more can your personal experiences be used to explain God to those you know? No one can argue with what you have experienced. Telling stories about what God has meant to you is one of the most powerful ways to attract others to believe in God too.

GOD'S CHALLENGE

Jesus said, "No, go home to your friends, and tell them what wonderful things the Lord has done for you and how merciful he has been." *Mark 5:19*

EVANGELISM

How can I overcome my fear of witnessing?

GOD'S RESPONSE

Now go, and do as I have told you. I will help you speak well, and I will tell you what to say.   *Exodus 4:12*

I will give you the right words and such wisdom that none of your opponents will be able to reply!   *Luke 21:15*

If you are asked about your Christian hope, always be ready to explain it.   *1 Peter 3:15*

FIRST, TAKE TIME TO STUDY the gospel message so you can be sure of what you believe and of how to explain it to others. This foundation will allow you to live your whole life as a convincing witness to others. When God prepares an opportunity for you to share your faith, you can be sure that he will also equip you with the words that you need. Just continue to surprise people by loving them in unexpected ways and then be willing to explain why you do.

GOD'S PROMISE

Do not tremble; do not be afraid. Have I not proclaimed from ages past what my purposes are for you? You are my witnesses—is there any other God? No! There is no other Rock—not one!   *Isaiah 44:8*

PLANTING SEEDS

What should I do when people aren't interested in hearing about Jesus?

GOD'S RESPONSE

My job was to plant the seed in your hearts, and Apollos watered it, but it was God, not we, who made it grow. *1 Corinthians 3:6*

You must give them my messages whether they listen or not. *Ezekiel 2:7*

S OMETIMES YOUR ROLE WILL SIMPLY be to plant a seed. Your job isn't to make people believe—only the Holy Spirit can soften and prepare people's hearts. Continue to live out what you believe and begin by building initial relationships with those who need to hear about Jesus. Trust God to prepare them and to provide the opportunity to share his love.

GOD'S PROMISE

If you give even a cup of cold water to one of the least of my followers, you will surely be rewarded. *Matthew 10:42*

AVAILABILITY

How can I make myself more available for God's use?

GOD'S RESPONSE

The LORD came and called as before, "Samuel! Samuel!"
And Samuel replied, "Yes, your servant is listening."
1 Samuel 3:10

I heard the Lord asking, "Whom should I send as a messenger to my people? Who will go for us?"
And I said, "Lord, I'll go! Send me." *Isaiah 6:8*

BEING AVAILABLE FOR SOMEONE means that you are prepared and willing to offer help. Being available to God includes the continual development of the gifts he has given you so that you will be prepared for him to use you. It then involves the willingness to use those gifts to serve him in the calling he currently has for you. Do you know the unique gifts God has given you? If not, take a spiritual gifts assessment and ask your friends what they think your gifts are.

GOD'S PROMISE

If you keep yourself pure, you will be a utensil God can use for his purpose. Your life will be clean, and you will be ready for the Master to use you for every good work.
2 Timothy 2:21

INSECURITY

How can I overcome the insecurities that get in the way of allowing God to use me?

GOD'S RESPONSE

We are God's masterpiece. He has created us anew in Christ Jesus, so that we can do the good things he planned for us long ago.   *Ephesians 2:10*

I can do everything with the help of Christ who gives me the strength I need.   *Philippians 4:13*

G OD MADE YOU IN HIS OWN IMAGE, so he must value you highly! He created you with unique gifts so you can do the specific tasks he has for you to do. He does not expect more from you than you can give, but he does expect you to use what he has given you. That's why it is so important to discover your own special gifts. When you match your unique God-given gifts with the right area of service, your insecurities will melt away and you will become bold in serving God. Then service will no longer be a chore, but a joy and passion.

GOD'S PROMISE

It is the one and only Holy Spirit who distributes these gifts. He alone decides which gift each person should have.   *1 Corinthians 12:11*

BEHAVIOR

What kind of behavior serves God best?

GOD'S RESPONSE

You should behave . . . like God's very own children.
Romans 8:15

Let your good deeds shine out for all to see, so that everyone
will praise your heavenly Father.   *Matthew 5:16*

Be kind to each other, tenderhearted, forgiving one
another, just as God through Christ has forgiven you.
Ephesians 4:32

O UR FAMILIES OFTEN HAVE distinct characteristics,
sometimes so much so that a person meeting us for the
first time can guess which family we belong to if they know
another member of our family. Your lifestyle also reflects
upon your heavenly family. As part of God's family, your
behaviors reflect back on him and may be used by others to
decide what they believe about God, so take your behavior
seriously and do your best to glorify your father in heaven.

GOD'S CHALLENGE

It isn't enough just to have faith. Faith that doesn't show
itself by good deeds is no faith at all—it is dead and
useless.   *James 2:17*

ATTITUDE

What kinds of attitudes does God want from me?

GOD'S RESPONSE

Your attitude should be the same that Christ Jesus had. *Philippians 2:5*

Always be joyful. Keep on praying. No matter what happens, always be thankful, for this is God's will for you who belong to Christ Jesus. *1 Thessalonians 5:16-18*

WHILE OTHERS WILL KNOW YOU ARE a Christian by your actions, God seems especially concerned with your attitudes, probably because your attitudes reflect your heart. Since you are called to be joyful and thankful, your attitudes are not always directly linked to your current emotional condition. Rather, your attitude is a choice of direction. You have complete confidence that you are moving toward eternal life in heaven—no wonder your attitude is one of joy and gratitude.

GOD'S PROMISE

The Kingdom of God is not a matter of what we eat or drink, but of living a life of goodness and peace and joy in the Holy Spirit. If you serve Christ with this attitude, you will please God. *Romans 14:17-18*

CHRISTLIKENESS

What does it mean to become like Christ?

GOD'S RESPONSE

I myself no longer live, but Christ lives in me.
Galatians 2:20

All of us have had that veil removed so that we can be mirrors that brightly reflect the glory of the Lord. And as the Spirit of the Lord works within us, we become more and more like him and reflect his glory even more.
2 Corinthians 3:18

WHEN WE LIVE WITH PEOPLE, we sometimes become like them. We adopt certain figures of speech or have accents like theirs. We sometimes begin to dress alike, or even think the way they do. The same is true when we live with Christ in us. Soon, our speech becomes gentle and kind, our face mirrors his joy, our attitudes and motives become more pure, and our actions are more service oriented. Can others tell that Christ lives in you?

GOD'S PROMISE

I am sure that God, who began the good work within you, will continue his work until it is finally finished on that day when Christ Jesus comes back again.
Philippians 1:6

FORGIVENESS

How can I become better at forgiving others?

GOD'S RESPONSE

Jesus said, "Father, forgive these people, because they don't know what they are doing." *Luke 23:34*

When you are praying, first forgive anyone you are holding a grudge against, so that your Father in heaven will forgive your sins, too. *Mark 11:25*

FORGIVENESS IS RARELY EASY. Humility and compassion are necessary if you want to accomplish it. First, it's important to remember the sins you have committed that God has already forgiven, simply because he loves you and has given you mercy. In reality, your sins and those of every other human being make you individually responsible for Jesus' sacrifice on the cross. Second, remember that many people are simply lost and don't know what they are doing. Though they may not deserve it, they still need your compassion and forgiveness.

GOD'S CHALLENGE

You must make allowance for each other's faults and forgive the person who offends you. Remember, the Lord forgave you, so you must forgive others.
Colossians 3:13

INTEGRITY

How does Jesus model integrity?

GOD'S RESPONSE

[Pilate] announced his verdict. "You brought this man to me, accusing him of leading a revolt. I have examined him thoroughly on this point in your presence and find him innocent. Herod came to the same conclusion and sent him back to us. Nothing this man has done calls for the death penalty." *Luke 23:14-15*

INTEGRITY MEANS KNOWING what you believe and living as though you believe it. No one is a better model of this than Jesus. Though we can never be perfect as he was, we can always grow in integrity. This involves being faithful in every area of your life, no matter how small. In fact, you'll probably find that it is in the small things that your integrity will be tested the most.

GOD'S CHALLENGE

Unless you are faithful in small matters, you won't be faithful in large ones. If you cheat even a little, you won't be honest with greater responsibilities. *Luke 16:10*

DENY YOURSELF

How do I deny myself and put others first as Jesus did?

GOD'S RESPONSE

If you try to keep your life for yourself, you will lose it. But if you give up your life for my sake and for the sake of the Good News, you will find true life. And how do you benefit if you gain the whole world but lose your own soul in the process? Is anything worth more than your soul? If a person is ashamed of me and my message in these adulterous and sinful days, I, the Son of Man, will be ashamed of that person when I return.   *Mark 8:35-38*

TO DENY YOURSELF DOESN'T MEAN you can't have or enjoy anything; instead, it means that you put Jesus first and others next. Put aside anything that gets in the way of that. Jesus understood that it is fundamentally fulfilling to live in service to others and that living only for yourself will lead to emptiness and disappointment. To have JOY, put Jesus first, Others second, and Yourself last.

GOD'S CHALLENGE

The greatest love is shown when people lay down their lives for their friends.   *John 15:13*

DEVOTION

How can I be totally devoted to Jesus, as the disciples were?

GOD'S RESPONSE

Jesus called out to them, "Come, be my disciples, and I will show you how to fish for people!" And they left their nets at once and went with him.   *Matthew 4:19-20*

T HE CALL AND PROMISE OF JESUS are striking but are powerless without our response. If Peter and Andrew had merely listened and said, "That's a very interesting invitation; maybe we can talk about it again after fishing season," they would not have become Jesus' disciples. They would have missed life on earth and in heaven with the greatest person who ever lived and who was also the God of the universe. You have that same choice with that same Jesus. What you decide now affects your life now and for eternity. Are you willing to sacrifice anything to follow him? You must make the decision—to follow him wherever he leads, or to remain where you are. The disciples left their nets and went after Jesus. Without a decision and action, devotion is just an interesting idea.

GOD'S PROMISE

Protect me, for I am devoted to you. Save me, for I serve you and trust you. You are my God.   *Psalm 86:2*

HUMILITY

How can I be more humble, as Christ was humble?

GOD'S RESPONSE

In human form he obediently humbled himself even further by dying a criminal's death on a cross.   *Philippians 2:8*

Rejoice greatly, O people of Zion! Shout in triumph, O people of Jerusalem! Look, your king is coming to you. He is righteous and victorious, yet he is humble, riding on a donkey—even on a donkey's colt.   *Zechariah 9:9*

Anyone who becomes as humble as this little child is the greatest in the Kingdom of Heaven.   *Matthew 18:4*

HUMILITY IS HONEST RECOGNITION of your worth as God sees you. Pride elevates us above others, and often above God himself. To destroy your sense of self-worth is also unacceptable, for it denies the value God placed upon you when he created you in his image. Jesus died for all people, so every person is greatly loved by him and has great worth in his eyes. Your goal is to see yourself as God sees you.

GOD'S PROMISE

You rescue those who are humble, but you humiliate the proud.   *Psalm 18:27*

SERVICE

How can I become more Christlike in the way I serve others?

GOD'S RESPONSE

Even I, the Son of Man, came here not to be served but to serve others, and to give my life as a ransom for many. *Matthew 20:28*

Since I, the Lord and Teacher, have washed your feet, you ought to wash each other's feet. I have given you an example to follow. *John 13:14-15*

A POPULAR NOTION OF SUCCESS is being able to afford the luxury of hiring others to keep your lawn, wash your car, or clean your house—in other words, to be served. Jesus turns this thinking on its head by teaching that the highest goal in life is not being served but being a servant. The reason he places such a high value on serving is that it is others-centered rather than self-centered. Service is the essence of a life modeled after Christ.

GOD'S CHALLENGE

You have been called to live in freedom—not freedom to satisfy your sinful nature, but freedom to serve one another in love. *Galatians 5:13*

COMPASSION

How can I be more Christlike in compassion for others?

GOD'S RESPONSE

They left by boat for a quieter spot. But many people saw them leaving, and people from many towns ran ahead along the shore and met them as they landed. A vast crowd was there as he stepped from the boat, and he had compassion on them because they were like sheep without a shepherd. *Mark 6:32-34*

COMPASSION IS BOTH AN EMOTION (we are moved with pity for someone) and an action (acting kindly to those in need). In many ways, compassion is a litmus test of our commitment and desire to love others as Christ loves us. If we are not moved by the incredible needs and hurts around us, we are developing hearts of stone, which will soon become too hard to respond to others. To be Christlike is also to share in his compassionate feelings and his response toward the needy, particularly those who cannot help themselves.

GOD'S PROMISE

The LORD is good to everyone. He showers compassion on all his creation. *Psalm 145:9*

LAMB OF GOD

Why is Jesus called the "Lamb of God"?

GOD'S RESPONSE

Abraham looked up and saw a ram caught by its horns in a bush. So he took the ram and sacrificed it as a burnt offering on the altar in place of his son.   *Genesis 22:13*

T HE SACRIFICIAL SYSTEM in the Old Testament, before the time of Jesus, reminded people of the seriousness of sin before their holy God. The offering of a sacrifice symbolized the person's desire to be forgiven for sin and thus to be restored to fellowship with God. In Old Testament times, a life had to be given up (usually a lamb's) so that a life could be spared (the person's). The blood of the sacrificed animal represented one life being poured out in substitution for another. This idea of a "substitute" foreshadowed Jesus' death on the cross for our sins. As the animal died so the sinner wouldn't have to, Jesus died so we wouldn't have to (Romans 5:6-11). The good news is that Jesus rose from the dead. His power over death guarantees his promise that we will also rise from the dead.

GOD'S PROMISE

He paid for you with the precious lifeblood of Christ, the sinless, spotless Lamb of God.   *1 Peter 1:19*

HEALING

Will Jesus heal the hurts in my life?

GOD'S RESPONSE

Moved with pity, Jesus touched him. "I want to," he said. "Be healed!"   *Mark 1:41*

For you who fear my name, the Sun of Righteousness will rise with healing in his wings. And you will go free, leaping with joy like calves let out to pasture.   *Malachi 4:2*

H E WHO MADE YOUR BODY can certainly repair and restore it. He who made your mind can repair and restore it. He who made your soul can repair it or restore it. Prayer is a powerful source of healing because it connects you with your creator. You know from God's Word that he loved you enough to die for you. He promises that in eternity you will be fully healed.

GOD'S PROMISE

I heard a loud shout from the throne, saying, "Look, the home of God is now among his people! He will live with them, and they will be his people. . . . He will remove all of their sorrows, and there will be no more death or sorrow or crying or pain."   *Revelation 21:3-4*

GOD'S SON

Why did God have to give his Son as a sacrifice for us?

GOD'S RESPONSE

A child is born to us, a son is given to us. *Isaiah 9:6*

For God so loved the world that he gave his only Son, so that everyone who believes in him will not perish but have eternal life. *John 3:16*

I F YOU ARE A PARENT, you know that you would do anything for your child's welfare, even to the point of death. To save your child's life, you would gladly give up your own. Yet God did the unthinkable—he gave up his only child! He purposely and willingly sent Jesus to earth to live as a human, and to experience the same joy and pain as we do. But then he was tortured and crucified and punished for our sins so we wouldn't have to experience that. Could you make this ultimate sacrifice of love? Don't let such lavish love be wasted. Accept God's gift of salvation and embrace the Christ child with all your heart.

GOD'S PROMISE

God showed how much he loved us by sending his only Son into the world so that we might have eternal life through him. This is real love. *1 John 4:9-10*

WONDERFUL COUNSELOR

How is Jesus my counselor?

GOD'S RESPONSE

A child is born to us, a son is given to us. . . . These will be his royal titles: Wonderful Counselor.   *Isaiah 9:6*

True wisdom and power are with God; counsel and understanding are his.   *Job 12:13*

Who can know what the Lord is thinking? Who can give him counsel? But we can understand these things, for we have the mind of Christ.   *1 Corinthians 2:16*

I F YOU ARE FORTUNATE, you have someone in your life that you can always depend on for advice. You are blessed when that person is not only wise and godly, but loving and caring as well, and always willing to give you as much time as you need. Jesus is such a counselor. He came for the purpose of giving you loving, caring, perfect counsel that will carry you through life and into eternity.

GOD'S PROMISE

I will send you the Counselor—the Spirit of truth. He will come to you from the Father and will tell you all about me.   *John 15:26*

MIGHTY GOD

How can a tiny baby be the mighty God?

GOD'S RESPONSE

A child is born to us, a son is given to us. . . . These will be his royal titles . . . Mighty God.   *Isaiah 9:6*

Suddenly, a terrible storm came up. . . . [Jesus] stood up and rebuked the wind and waves, and suddenly all was calm. The disciples just sat there in awe. "Who is this?" they asked themselves. "Even the wind and waves obey him!"   *Matthew 8:24, 26-27*

I depend on Christ's mighty power that works within me. *Colossians 1:29*

I T'S HARD TO PICTURE THE BABY JESUS as the mighty God, but he was mighty enough to create the world, live a sinless life, heal countless people, calm storms, and conquer death. He is mighty enough to conquer your troubles too!

GOD'S PROMISE

By his mighty power at work within us, he is able to accomplish infinitely more than we would ever dare to ask or hope.   *Ephesians 3:20*

PEACE WITHIN

How can I find peace within?

GOD'S RESPONSE

I will lie down in peace and sleep, for you alone, O Lord, will keep me safe. *Psalm 4:8*

The Lord gives his people strength. The Lord blesses them with peace. *Psalm 29:11*

For you are my hiding place; you protect me from trouble. You surround me with songs of victory. *Psalm 32:7*

Y OU CAN HAVE PEACE WITHIN, in spite of your circumstances, when you fully trust that God is always watching over your soul. The peace of God will not prevent you from encountering difficulties, but will give you victory over them. God promises to give you eternal life in a perfect heaven, and he promises that Satan cannot steal your soul away from God. When you have total confidence in these two things, then no matter what happens, you can have peace with God.

GOD'S PROMISE

He who watches over Israel never tires and never sleeps.
Psalm 121:4

PRINCE OF PEACE

How does Jesus bring peace into my life?

GOD'S RESPONSE

Don't be troubled. You trust God, now trust in me.
John 14:1

You will keep in perfect peace all who trust in you, whose
thoughts are fixed on you!   *Isaiah 26:3*

THERE ARE SO MANY THINGS that affect peace: chaos,
conflict, interruptions, wars, busyness, worry, fear.
How can we have peace from all that? On this earth, you
can't prevent many of these things from invading your life,
but you can have peace—a quiet, unshakable confidence—
about the outcome. How do some people have such peace
just before they are martyred for their faith in Jesus? They
know where they are going. If you had ten million dollars
in the bank, you wouldn't worry about providing for your
family if you lost your job. In the same way, if you have
banked treasure in heaven, you don't worry about losing
your life on earth. Let that assurance keep you from panick-
ing in today's storms. The outcome is certain.

GOD'S PROMISE

On earth you will have many trials and sorrows. But take
heart, because I have overcome the world.   *John 16:33*

JESUS' BIRTH

Why was Jesus' birth so odd?

GOD'S RESPONSE

Remember, dear brothers and sisters, that few of you were wise in the world's eyes, or powerful, or wealthy when God called you. Instead, God deliberately chose things the world considers foolish in order to shame those who think they are wise. And he chose those who are powerless to shame those who are powerful.   *1 Corinthians 1:26-27*

GOD OFTEN ACCOMPLISHES his purposes in unexpected ways. God used the census of a heathen emperor to bring Joseph and Mary to Bethlehem. Maybe that is also why he chose to have Jesus born in a stable rather than a palace, why he chose Bethlehem rather than Jerusalem, and why the news of Jesus' birth went first to shepherds rather than to kings. God may have done all this to show that life's greatest treasure—salvation through Jesus—is available to all. And it may also show that the lowly and humble might have a better chance of receiving that message.

GOD'S PROMISE

God blesses those who are humble, for they will inherit the whole earth.   *Matthew 5:5 (NLT2)*

INCARNATION

Why did God choose to send his Son into the world as a baby?

GOD'S RESPONSE

God in his gracious kindness declares us not guilty. He has done this through Christ Jesus, who has freed us by taking away our sins. For God sent Jesus to take the punishment for our sins.   *Romans 3:24-25*

GOD'S MISSION WAS TO save us for eternity and to show us how to live now. The Incarnation (the Son of God coming to us "in the flesh") means that God, in the form of a human baby, entered into our world to identify with our situation, to experience our suffering, and to suffer for our salvation. We can never claim that God doesn't understand, because God stood where we stand. Refusing to stand aloof or apart from us, the Lord entered fully into our lives (read Hebrews 2:14-18). As one of us, yet one who is also fully divine, he was able to pay the full price for our sin, opening the way to eternal life. He is also able to show us how to live a life of surrender and obedience to God.

GOD'S PROMISE

For God so loved the world that he gave his only Son, so that everyone who believes in him will not perish but have eternal life.   *John 3:16*

RESPONDING TO JESUS

What should our response be to Jesus?

GOD'S RESPONSE

They entered the house and saw the child . . . and they bowed down and worshiped him.   *Matthew 2:11 (NLT2)*

We praise God for the wonderful kindness he has poured out on us because we belong to his dearly loved Son. *Ephesians 1:6*

"My Lord and my God!" Thomas exclaimed.   *John 20:28*

THE ASTROLOGERS TRAVELED THOUSANDS of miles to see the king of the Jews. When they finally found him, they responded with joy, worship, and gifts. How different from the approach we often take today! We expect God to come looking for us, explain himself, prove who he is, and give us gifts. Those who are wise still seek Jesus because they suspect that he was sent for a special purpose unlike that of any other person. Do you really know who he is? What gift can you give back to Jesus, who gave his life for you?

GOD'S PROMISE

Look! Here I stand at the door and knock. If you hear me calling and open the door, I will come in, and we will share a meal as friends.   *Revelation 3:20*

REFLECTION

How can I keep Christmas alive all year long?

GOD'S RESPONSE

Mary quietly treasured these things in her heart and thought about them often.   *Luke 2:19*

Praise the LORD, I tell myself, and never forget the good things he does for me.   *Psalm 103:2*

CHRISTMAS IS OVER, and all the secrets are out. The gifts have been opened, the feast devoured, the songs sung, the joy celebrated. Today is a good day to take some time to reflect, as Mary did more than 2,000 years ago, on the events of the big day, on the gifts that were given, and on the love that was bestowed. Store the good times and memories away in your heart so you can think about and smile over them in the weeks and months ahead. Reflect on the goodness of God, who gave the best gift of all—his Son. Commit yourself to sharing the story of Christmas all year long.

GOD'S CHALLENGE

We will not hide these truths from our children but will tell the next generation about the glorious deeds of the LORD. We will tell of his power and the mighty miracles he did.   *Psalm 78:4*

REGRETS

As this year ends, I have some regrets.
How do I deal with them?

GOD'S RESPONSE

Forgetting the past and looking forward to what lies ahead, I strain to reach the end of the race and receive the prize for which God, through Christ Jesus, is calling us up to heaven.   *Philippians 3:13-14*

Those who become Christians become new persons. They are not the same anymore, for the old life is gone. A new life has begun!   *2 Corinthians 5:17*

A S YOU APPROACH THE END OF THE YEAR, it's natural to look back and reflect on different events. Some memories bring smiles, but others bring regret. Now is a good time to clean house—to confess your shortcomings to God, to apologize and make amends to those you have wronged, and then to leave the pain behind. Forget the failures of the past and move forward into the new year with expectation and excitement.

GOD'S PROMISE

If we confess our sins to him, he is faithful and just to forgive us and to cleanse us from every wrong.
1 John 1:9

FINISHING WELL

How can I plan to finish well next year?

GOD'S RESPONSE

The master was full of praise. "Well done, my good
and faithful servant. You have been faithful in handling
this small amount, so now I will give you many more
responsibilities. Let's celebrate together!" *Matthew 25:21*

Be sure to do what you should, for then you will enjoy
the personal satisfaction of having done your work well,
and you won't need to compare yourself to anyone else.
Galatians 6:4

IT'S ALMOST SCARY when another year has slipped by.
You wonder how it went by so quickly. That's why it's so
important to do your best each day, in your work, in your
relationships, in your walk with God, and even in your
rest. Be faithful to the responsibilities that God has given
you. Then, at year's end, you will have the satisfaction of
finishing a job well done. And God will be pleased as well.

GOD'S PROMISE

I am sure that God, who began the good work within
you, will continue his work until it is finally finished
on that day when Christ Jesus comes back again.
Philippians 1:6

PLANS

What must I do to prepare for the coming year?

GOD'S RESPONSE

Trust in the LORD with all your heart; do not depend on your own understanding. Seek his will in all you do, and he will direct your paths.   *Proverbs 3:5-6*

You can make many plans, but the LORD's purpose will prevail.   *Proverbs 19:21*

The LORD says, "I will guide you along the best pathway for your life. I will advise you and watch over you." *Psalm 32:8*

G OD ALREADY KNOWS what the next year will hold for you. He has some great plans for you. He will advise you and watch over you along the way. When you have asked for God's guidance and direction, you can move forward with confidence, knowing that his purpose and work will get done.

GOD'S PROMISE

We know that God causes everything to work together for the good of those who love God and are called according to his purpose for them.   *Romans 8:28*

FRESH START

How can I ensure that a year from now I will be better off?

GOD'S RESPONSE

He died for everyone so that those who receive his new life will no longer live to please themselves. Instead, they will live to please Christ, who died and was raised for them.   *2 Corinthians 5:15*

I advise you to live according to your new life in the Holy Spirit. Then you won't be doing what your sinful nature craves.   *Galatians 5:16*

THERE'S A WHOLE NEW YEAR just around the corner. It's a fresh start, with no mistakes yet. In a sense, this is your chance to become a new person. In the year ahead, commit to growing every day in your relationship with the Lord, even just a little bit. Ask the Holy Spirit to change you, day by day, into all God wants you to be. If you are changed for the better 365 times, you will be a much better person a year from now!

GOD'S PROMISE

Those who become Christians become new persons. They are not the same anymore, for the old life is gone. A new life has begun!   *2 Corinthians 5:17*

*What should I stop doing and what should I start
doing so I can begin the year well and end it well?*

GOD'S RESPONSE

Stop loving this evil world and all that it offers you.
1 John 2:15

Begin to understand the incredible greatness of his power
for us who believe him.   *Ephesians 1:19*

STOP LOOKING BACK WITH REGRET, stop thinking you
can't overcome a bad habit or addiction, stop thinking God doesn't care, stop blaming yourself or others,
stop doing what you know you shouldn't, stop doing too
much, stop doing too little. Start each day with God in
prayer and Bible reading, start showing more grace and
forgiveness, start a new good habit, start obeying God's
Word, start repairing hurt relationships, start trusting
God in your life every day. Remember that God is the
one constant that will never change.

GOD'S PROMISE

The LORD will guide you continually, watering your
life when you are dry and keeping you healthy, too. You
will be like a well-watered garden, like an ever-flowing
spring.   *Isaiah 58:11*

INDEX

Abilities — January 6
Absence — November 30
Abundance — July 16
Accountability — April 3
Alpha and Omega — December 31
Ambition — March 9, 10, 11
Anger — May 22
Answers — May 3
Approval — October 7
Armor — January 25
Assumptions — June 13
Attitude — December 7
Availability — December 4
Backsliding — September 10
Bad Habits — October 10
Battles — January 24, October 28
Behavior — December 6
Bible — February 1
Blessings — March 7
Boomerang — October 8
Burdens — November 7
Burnout — October 24, 25
Business — June 7
Calling — January 8
Caution — January 17
Celebration — October 20
Challenges — March 15, November 21, 22

Chance — August 14
Change — March 16, July 25, August 3
Character — March 17, August 29, 30
Childlikeness — September 3
Choices — July 31
Christlikeness — December 8
Church — August 25, 26
Circumstances — July 26
Cleansing — October 15
Commitment — October 19, November 12
Communication — May 4, 6
Comparisons — June 12
Compassion — December 15
Competition — June 10, 11
Complaining — June 22
Compliments — August 22
Compromise — June 23, October 9
Confession — February 27, May 9
Confidence — March 31
Conflict — August 17, November 8
Confrontation — April 4, 5
Connection — February 2
Conscience — July 1
Contentment — February 17, April 10, July 10
Courage — April 7, 8, 9
Criticism — August 20, 21

Cross	March 27	Forgiveness	February 28, March 1,
Danger	October 26		May 29, October 16,
Death	March 28		December 9
Decision-Making	July 30	Freedom	July 6
Decisions	March 18	Fresh Start	January 1, December 30
Defeat	August 11	Friendship	June 26, 27, 28, 29, 30
Defense	January 31	Gentleness	September 26, 27
Delegation	March 20	Giants	June 20
Delight	July 14	Giving	April 13, 19
Deny Yourself	December 11	Giving Your Best	October 3
Dependence	February 11	Goals	January 5, 7
Depression	August 10	God's Anger	October 5
Desires	August 1	God's Judgment	June 21
Devotion	December 12	God's Love	February 9, 10
Disconnection	October 4	God's Plan	October 21
Discontentment	October 18	God's Promises	April 23,
Discouragement	August 7, 8		November 3
Disrespect	September 28	God's Son	December 18
Distance	February 21	Goodness	September 20, 21
Distress	February 24,	Gossip	August 16
	April 26	Grace	October 13
Dysfunction	August 15	Gratitude	September 22
Employees	June 9	Happiness	July 15
Empowerment	May 8	Healing	December 17
Endurance	November 13	Heart	February 3, 6
Enemies	September 5	Heartbreak	February 8
Envy	August 4	Heroes	November 11
Escape	May 13	Hiding	March 8
Evangelism	December 2	Holiness	August 12
Example	March 19, 21, June 1	Holy Spirit	October 22
Expectations	August 5, 6	Honesty	May 25
Failure	March 2, 3	Hope	July 19, 20
Faith	April 28, October 12,	Humility	February 5, December 13
	November 10	Hypocrisy	June 2
Faithfulness	September 23, 24, 25	Impatience	September 15
Father	June 15	Impossibility	November 1, 2
Fear of God	April 27	Incarnation	December 24
Fellowship	August 27, 28	Influence	January 4
Finishing Well	December 28	Inner Conflict	August 18
Flattery	October 23	Insecurity	December 5
Foolishness	April 1, 2	Inspiration	March 14
Forgetting	July 22	Integrity	June 6, December 10

Intercession	July 29
Intimacy	February 15, 16
Jesus' Birth	December 23
Journey	January 10
Joy	September 6, 7
Joyfulness	September 8
Kindness	September 17, 18, 19
Lamb of God	December 16
Laziness	May 23
Leaders	July 5
Leadership	March 12, 13
Legacy	May 31
Listening	May 2
Love	February 13, 14, September 2, 4
Materialism	April 14
Memories	May 28
Mighty God	December 20
Money	April 12
Motivation	March 23
Motives	May 18, 19
Nearness	February 22
Needs	April 15
Neighbor	July 9
Newness	March 30
Obedience	May 7
Obstacles	November 16
Odds	November 6
Opposition	November 17, 18
Panic	April 16
Past	May 27
Patience	September 14
Peace	January 28, September 11, 13
Peace with God	September 12
Peace Within	December 21
Perspective	August 19, October 27
Plans	June 25, December 29
Planting Seeds	December 3
Pleasing God	July 13
Pleasure	July 12
Potential	September 9
Power	April 24, 25, June 16
Prayer	May 1, July 4
Preparation	November 9
Presence	February 19, 20
Pride	May 20, 21
Prince of Peace	December 22
Problems	April 30
Productivity	September 1
Provision	January 9, April 18, 21
Purification	November 28
Rationalization	March 22
Rebellion	June 24
Recovery	May 15
Reflection	August 31, December 26
Refreshment	July 10
Regrets	May 30, December 27
Relationship	February 12
Reliability	April 22
Remembrance	March 26
Repentance	October 6
Reputation	May 26
Rescuer	June 18
Resistance	May 14, August 2, November 5
Resources	November 15
Respect	August 23
Responding to Jesus	December 25
Responsibility	April 6, June 14
Rest	July 2, 3
Restlessness	July 24
Resurrection	March 29
Retirement	November 20
Right Living	October 11
Righteousness	January 27
Risk	January 14, 15, 16
Role Model	November 14
Routine	May 5, August 24
Salt	October 14
Salvation	January 22, 30
Satan	October 29
Scarcity	July 18
Second Chances	November 4

Self-Control	*September 30, October 1*
Servant Leadership	*March 24*
Service	*December 14*
Shield	*January 29*
Speaking Up	*November 19*
Spiritual Dryness	*August 9*
Spiritual Eyesight	*July 27*
Spiritual Warfare	*October 30, 31*
Stability	*July 28*
Strength	*April 29, July 8*
Substitution	*March 25*
Success	*March 4, 5, 6, April 20*
Suffering	*February 23, 25, 26, June 19*
Superstition	*July 11*
Supervision	*June 8*
Temptation	*May 11, 12, September 29*
Tenderness	*February 4*
Testimony	*December 1*
Thankfulness	*November 24, 25, 26, 27*
Thanks	*October 17, November 23*
Theft	*May 24*
Thoughts	*May 16, 17*
Time	*July 23*
Trouble	*April 17, November 29*
Trust	*January 13, 21, February 7*
Truth	*January 26*
Uncertainty	*January 11*
Victory	*August 13*
Vision	*January 2, 3*
Waiting	*July 21, September 16*
Warrior God	*January 23, June 17*
Wealth	*April 11*
Weariness	*July 7*
Wisdom	*January 18, 19, 20*
Wonderful Counselor	*December 19*
Words	*May 10, October 2*
Work	*June 3, 4, 5*
Worry	*January 12*
Worship	*February 18*